Morality and Youth:
Fostering Christian Identity

James DiGiacomo, S.J.

Sheed & Ward

Sheed & Ward is a service of The National Catholic Reporter Publishing Company.

Library of Congress Cataloguing in Publication Data

DiGiacomo, James.
    Morality and youth : fostering Christian identity / James DiGiacomo
      p.   cm.
    Includes bibliographical references.
    ISBN 1-55612-652-2 (alk. paper)
    1. Church work with youth--Catholic Church. 2. Christian education of teenagers. 3. Teenagers--Religious life. 4. Moral education (Secondary) 5. Catholic Church--Education. I. Title.
BX2347.8.Y7D54 1993
286′.433′08822--dc20   93-938
                                                  CIP

Published by: Sheed & Ward
                    115 E. Armour Blvd.
                    P.O. Box 419492
                    Kansas City, MO 64141-6492

To order, call: (800) 333-7373

Contents

Foreword

THE RELIGIOUS AND MORAL EDUCATION OF YOUNG PEOPLE HAS always been an enterprise of great interest to adult members of the Roman Catholic Church. Even the realization that the continuing education of adults is at least as important if not more so, has not diminished a healthy concern with the growth of the next generation. For the future of the church, after all, belongs to them. So it is that, in every era, we must ask ourselves how faithfully and effectively we are telling our children the story of our tribe and helping them to become part of that story when they take our places.

This book is an attempt to put to religious educators and others in youth ministry the question that the mayor of a large city used frequently to ask his constituents: "How am I doin'?" How are we doing in the difficult but vital task of handing on the faith to our young? The decades following the Second Vatican Council have seen extraordinary changes, fluctuations, experiments, backtracking, and reappraisals of the way we talk with our children of the things of God. Many are convinced that these developments, both positive and negative, were necessary to avoid stagnation and to meet the needs of a new generation. Others survey with dismay what they perceive as wreckage and betrayal.

My own feeling is that the catechetical revolution of the last half of the twentieth century was inevitable, partly successful, and partly a failure. Even the most optimistic will admit that there is a good deal of unfinished business. What follows is a collection of writings on this subject over the past several years. These try to put in perspective the events and developments of the postconciliar decades and to take a reading on our present course. As we move toward the end of this century, what are our prospects for sharing our faith with the first adults of the next millennium?

How are we doin'?

iv

Chapter 1

The New Illiteracy

ONE OF THE BIG RELIGIOUS NEWS STORIES OF RECENT YEARS WAS the publication, in 1993, of the new universal catechism. Its authors, who had been engaged in the project for several years, were responding to what many perceived as an alarming degree of religious illiteracy among church members. To no one's surprise, it prompted mixed reactions from concerned adults. Many in youth ministry and in religious education of the young fear that a document too narrowly conceived and executed may stifle creativity and quench the Spirit. They warn that a good deal of wheat may be lost along with the chaff. On the other hand, those who promoted the project and rejoiced in its completion are concerned with a very real problem in the church. They hope that they have the cure for the present epidemic of ignorance about things religious and an antidote for lukewarmness and apathy, especially among the young. But this formula, whatever the ailment it wants to treat, may leave untouched a much more serious affliction.

To be sure, children and young people do suffer from disconcerting and even alarming deficiencies in their grasp of Christian doctrine. They always have. Religious illiteracy is not a phenomenon peculiar to the post-Vatican II church. Even in the not-so-good old preconciliar days, in the heyday of the Baltimore Catechism, youngsters exhibited a tenacious propensity to forget what they had been taught. In the decade that followed the council, there was less to forget because they were being taught less, as many school programs became alarmingly thin on content. This in turn spawned the back-to-basics movement of the late seventies that was not always reactionary and which had some positive effects. Publishers of religion textbooks made a genuine effort to beef up their offerings with challenging doctrinal content, and many schools did the same for their curricula. So things have gotten better with the swing of the pendulum toward academic seriousness. Still, the question remains: What's wrong with giving children correct religious information and hence greater religious literacy? And will the universal catechism help achieve it?

The Real Problem

The answer to the second question is probably no, because the first question is misconceived. Of course, it is desirable that young people be well informed. They need to understand and appreciate what Christians believe and value. They need to be familiar with the religious practices of our community, and to develop the skills of prayer and worship that are part of our way of life. To the extent that a catechism might contribute to these goals, it would be of real service to the church. And if indeed that should be the eventual outcome, this writer will cheerfully admit to having been wrong again. But the real problem will remain unsolved, because the kind of religious illiteracy that we are dealing with today is something new and will probably be untouched by any catechism, however successful.

To understand what this new and intractable illiteracy is, we have to go back a few steps and consider what has been going on in religious education and youth ministry in the last two decades. First, some good news. Those of us who minister to the young have learned a great deal about adapting to their needs. We have developed skills in communicating with the young. We have learned how to announce the gospel message not in a vacuum but in ways that speak to the young in their actual situation, in language and categories better suited to their stages of growth, with a more sophisticated awareness of their needs, limitations, and capacities. During these years youth ministry has come of age; a whole professional class has emerged, and new structures have been developed to reach youngsters where they are, rather than where we would like them to be. Like good missionaries, we have learned how to adapt to the natives, to respect their (youth) culture, to listen to and take seriously both them and their experience.

But there may be bad news as well. Missionaries must not only adapt to the natives they serve; they must also be faithful to the message they have come to proclaim. How well are we doing this? Are we helping produce a generation of disciples, or just turning out a different kind of religious consumer? To help us answer this question, consider the following checklist.

In our religious converse with the young, do we talk about Jesus' Father the way he does? In some ways, the answer is obviously yes. Children in today's church learn of God's love and care and of their own worth. But do they hear of a God who makes demands? Or does he come through as a God who wants whatever they want? We rightly teach them, as Jesus did, that God's love for us is unconditional, that he loves me no matter what I do. But what some may be hearing is, "God loves me so much, he doesn't care what I do."

What do we say about sin and repentance? Besides offering affirmation and encouragement and shoring up their self-image and sense of worth, do we help them deal with their failings— their selfishness, their destructiveness of self and others, their greed, their cruelty, their apathy?

In passing on Jesus' invitation to the kingdom and his offer of salvation, do we describe a game played for high stakes, or a game that no one can lose? What has happened to his sense of urgency?

Where is the idealism in the version of Christianity presently being offered? Does Christ's invitation come through as a call to greatness, a challenge to bring out the best that is in us? Do we say anything about the cross? And if we don't, are we running the risk of trivializing the gospel?

Are There Costs?

In inviting the young to be followers of Christ, do we spell out any concrete commitments? Are there requirements for church membership? To be a Catholic, is there anything concrete that you have to *do*? Is there anything, besides murder, rape, and terrorism, that you're *not* supposed to do? What is a practicing Catholic? Is the notion obsolete? In a time of religious consumerism, do we unwittingly encourage such a mentality by not making demands or offering challenges? If we don't put a price tag on discipleship, are we, in effect, offering cheap grace?

Every year, when the subject of hell comes up in my high school religion classes, I am predictably assured by a number of my students that no one is there. After telling them that I hope they are right, I ask them how they can be so sure. They explain, in various ways, that God loves everyone so much that we are all certain to make it. This kind of optimism is appealing but hard to square with innumerable passages in the New Testament, where Jesus warns us, in the most solemn terms, of the fate that awaits those who refuse his Father's offer of life. (Are these texts ever chosen as readings in the youth liturgy?) Monika Hellwig very aptly sums up this theme in Jesus' preaching: that everything is at stake in the way human beings use their freedom. How prominent is this theme in religious education and exhortation of the young?

If such hard sayings are neglected in youth catechesis, it is quite understandable. Most of those who teach children have long since lost their enthusiasm for trying to frighten them into being good. Our past record of stressing fear and guilt, often to excess, has prompted an enduring backlash among grown-ups who either remember or have heard of the bad old days. And youth ministers, keenly aware of adolescents' need for affirmation and positive motivation, are naturally uncomfortable in dealing with sin and guilt. Moreover, the teen years are, for many, a time of rebellion and rejection, indeed of estrangement from adults and adult institutions like church. It hardly looks like a time to make demands, to formulate rules, to call for decision and commitment. But what happens to the message of Christ when these elements are omitted or soft-pedaled? Is it still the same? Or have the missionaries unwittingly lost their way?

One of the missionaries who thinks they have is William O'Malley, a veteran religion teacher and writer:

> In reacting against the overly restrictive and punitive God many of us were introduced to in our childhood we have come full cycle in the other direction: from Moloch to Milquetoast. The God we encounter in homilies and in the hymns we mumble and moan on Sunday is almost exclusively the Good Shepherd who will pat our woolly heads and make everything nice and peaceful. . . .

> If the homilist dodges the thornier aspects and goes for the consoling, if he tries to make it look easy, effectively denying the very words of Christ that being a Christian means carrying a cross—daily—then the Gospel is made to appear flaccid [and] spineless. And so is Jesus.[1]

Are we still talking about religious illiteracy? Yes, but not of the kind that the new catechism will probably try to address. The problems described here go deeper than lack of information or of command of religious language and terminology. They will not be solved by formulas couched in question-and-answer formats, no matter how orthodox or theologically acute. The crisis is not one of verbalism but of vitality.

What Ails Them?

So far we have spoken of deficiencies in the ministers and their ministry, especially of the word. What about young people themselves, the hearers of the word, those to whom we minister? Is there any evidence among them of the accuracy or inaccuracy of the above diagnosis? Once again, it depends on where you look, on one's tendency to see vessels as half-empty or half-full. The religious scene among youth is a various one, with signs of great promise as well as of disappointment which should discourage extremes of optimism or pessimism. With these precautions in mind, consider the attitudes of many young Catholics to the sacramental life of the church, especially the Eucharist. They can be summed up in two complaints heard over and over again: "It's boring," and "I don't get anything out of it." Whether we like it or not, these two expressions tell us a great deal about the religion of young people.

The first thing to be said about boredom in church is that it is nothing new. What is new is that it is now offered as a serious reason for dropping out. The most charitable interpretation of this phenomenon is that it bespeaks a desire for well-celebrated liturgy and a dissatisfaction with poorly planned and executed worship. But surely that is not all. There are many things in life that we all keep doing, even in the face of boredom, because they are *important*. The desire for meaningful religious experience is laudable, but it does not account, all by itself, for the degree of neglect of the Eucharist by both young and old. The way people react to boredom reflects the value they place on certain things. For instance, good students are often bored by school, just as are their unsuccessful peers; but where the latter respond by dropping out, the former persevere. And it is not so much a matter of ability as it is of motivation: to them, learning is so important that they won't let even boredom deter them. In the same way, in other parts of the school, candidates for the football team endure mind-numbing drills and musicians on the school band put up with repetitive rehearsals. (By the way, would it be impertinent to suggest that, for some of us, boredom just might be the cross that we are asked to bear?)

Before leaving the subject of boredom, we should admit that there is another possible interpretation of this nagging phenomenon. It may be that religion is only part of a larger problem. Some think that churchgoing is but one of many casualties of people's need for stimulation and their intolerance of routine. How many relationships, how many projects and enterprises are abandoned because of flagging enthusiasm? Like children with short attention spans, we may as a people be suffering from a shrinking capacity for commitment and its offspring, perseverance. In this gloomy scenario, our young are the forerunners of a new and not necessarily better culture in which many more things besides religion will suffer. And their absence from church would then be the tip of a much larger iceberg.

The second reason offered for the nonpractice of religion is "'I don't get anything out of it." Religious people are tempted to dismiss such an excuse with impatience, or to treat it as dishonest. But it deserves a closer look. What do they mean by "getting something out of it"? The best way to find out is by asking them about good experiences—times when worship and prayer have been perceived as rewarding or worthwhile. The answers are so predictable as to be quite revealing. The same replies are heard over and over again: "We had a feeling of real closeness." "There was a very peaceful atmosphere." "People weren't phony; they were being themselves." "I came out feeling much better about myself." "We had a sense of coming together, of opening up." What these reactions have in common is an *immediate, perceptible, emotional* return on their investment of time and attention. Such results are always gratifying and desirable, of course; we all need them, at least from time to time. But they are not the only, or even the most important, indication of the worth of our religious activities. Often the really significant effects of our efforts at prayer and worship are not perceived until much later, after long bouts of plodding, dogged effort. Indeed, this is true of many other areas in our lives, when the fruits of our perseverance take long to bloom but outlast flashier but less enduring results.

The preoccupation of many young people with immediate, perceptible evidence of religious effectiveness is disturbing because when such evidence is lacking, the religious activities are seen as futile and to be abandoned as worthless. This is a very serious pastoral problem, and it arises from a kind of religious illiteracy. What we have here is a very limited understanding of spiritual realities in general, and an impoverished notion, in particular, of what sacraments are all about. There is an enduring conviction in Christian tradition that God is present to us in privileged ways in sacramental encounters; that his action on our behalf is efficacious even when our response is limited by distraction or any other obstacle proceeding from our human weakness and sinfulness. True, God does not force himself on us; but the divine initiative is not totally conditioned, much less cancelled, by our limitations. This is not to be construed as a whitewash of perfunctory, careless, or uninspired celebrations, but as an attempt to recover some valuable things in Catholic tradition that are in danger of being lost. When traditions are ignored, it is people, more than institutions, that are impoverished.

From several angles I have been describing a kind of religious illiteracy that goes far beyond the inability to rattle off orthodox answers to theological questions or to master lists of commandments, capital sins, names of apostles, and gifts of the Holy Spirit. It has to do with matters of greater moment—images of God, fidelity to Jesus' message, attitudes toward prayer and worship, and grasp of fundamental sacramental theology.

Will the new catechism help us meet these challenges? Let us hope so. But I doubt that it can have a significant impact on the current religious culture. Our needs, and the needs of our young people, lie elsewhere. We need a more authentically Christian notion of what religion is all about. We have to help them recover a sense of measuring up to something or someone, or their religiosity will degenerate into a new narcissism. Adolescents, especially, need assistance in dealing with some perennial questions that still await answers: What is God like, and what does he want from me? Is Jesus any more than a pal? How do I deal with my sinfulness? Can I accept a church of imperfect people and find a place in it? How do I reconcile my desire for spontaneity with a realistic acceptance and even esteem of routine? Do sacramental celebrations have any worth when they do not issue in immediate, palpable self-improvement?

Teach What Jesus Taught

If the above diagnosis of the present religious situation is at all accurate, then there is no quick fix We all have a lot of work to do to improve the quality of religious education. We can begin by talking about a God who is transcendent as well as immanent; whose ways are not always our ways; who makes demands. Like Jesus, we should tell them not only that his Father loves them but that he has high expectations of them.

Talk about sin, and don't just call it a failure to love. Sin always has a name, whether it be greed or cruelty or selfishness or apathy or stealing or sexual irresponsibility. Tell them that forgiveness is available, but on condition that we acknowledge our faults and try to change our ways. This may belabor the obvious, but a more than casual observer of the youth scene can be struck by how seldom such things are spoken of.

When planning the youth retreat talks or choosing the readings for liturgies, see if there is any sense of urgency or challenge, or if the same consoling generalities are repeated over and over again. Is anything ever said about the cross? Does anyone ever mention sacrifice and self-denial? Jesus had a way of dropping oneliners that left even his closest followers aghast. When was the last time your kids were surprised that way?

Somewhere along the line, we ought to talk with youngsters about the difference between cultural and practicing Catholics. This can emerge in our teaching about sacraments if we go beyond vague generalities. One of the most glaring weaknesses in contemporary Catholic life, among adults and youth, is neglect of the sacraments. There is no easy solution to this problem, but not talking about it will not make it go away.

None of this will happen unless we adults are clear about who we are and what we believe. The shortcomings of youthful religious belief and practice are a function of a crisis of identity in the larger community.

Until the shepherds get together, we can hardly expect the sheep to follow. Even with a catechism to show the way.

Topics for Discussion

1. This chapter speaks of disciples, religious consumers, cultural and practising Catholics. How would you define or describe these types?

2. Do you see any evidence, among young and/or old, of a shrinking capacity for commitment in nonreligious matters?

3. Does this sound like a call to return to the bad old days of religious education and formation?

Notes

1. "Jesus the Warm Fuzzy," *America*, March 15, 1986, p. 205.

Chapter 2

Teaching the Next New Breed

IF GEORGE SANTAYANA WAS CORRECT IN SAYING THAT THOSE WHO ignore history are condemned to repeat it, then, before we set out to improve the quality of religious education and formation, we would do well to examine our recent history in greater detail. What were the events and developments in the postconciliar church that brought us to the present crisis?

One of the big religious stories of the 1970's that continued into the nineties was the gradual reawakening of youth to religious concerns—a new openness, on their part, to religious experience and commitment. Mystery and prayer were "in" again. God's stock has gone up once more on the campus and in the schoolyard. Religious educators and youth ministers sense a genuine opportunity to share the Christian message with the young. There is a feeling that, despite all the problems that still face us, the fields are white for the harvest.

In its own way, the cult phenomenon reinforced this perception. An experienced deprogrammer, Rabbi Maurice Davis, observed that cults were offering what many young people were looking for: involvement, support, and a sense of belonging. In case you didn't notice, that's what the church of Jesus Christ is supposed to offer, too.

So God is alive and well among our young people who are seeking Him or Her with a seriousness and urgency that were rare in the sixties and early seventies. The Great American Dream of a consumer paradise built for hedonists and materialists has a bad name among the young. Many of our children hunger for something more. They long for some kind of idealism; they want to serve something bigger than themselves. They have long since tired of freedom without direction. They sense that self-indulgence without commitment to some larger meaning will lead to a dead end. Of course, they are very ambivalent about all this. Even as they decry the shallowness of materialism, they hurry to buy the latest junk that's "in" this year. Even as they complain about the pressures of conformity, they give in to them. While they profess to reject hedonism as a way of life, their actions betray the confusion in their priorities. Even as they reach for goals and ideals, they are scared to death that they might not look cool in front of their friends. In all this, of course, they are much like their elders. Welcome, boys and girls, to the human condition!

But they'd like to do better. And they can, with a little help from us. How can we help? Among other things, we can and must develop a style of religious education for the rest of this century that will seize the opportunities that present themselves to us now and in the next few years. Catholic schools and youth programs must help turn out a new kind of Catholic for the 21st century: Christian humanists who have been effectively evangelized, who know their faith and are open to Gospel values. A new style of catechesis must evolve, if the next generation of Catholics is to be committed to church renewal and the transformation of society. It must be at once faithful to authentic Christian tradition, and attuned to the religious mentality of the young. I suggest that to accomplish these goals will be possible but quite difficult, for there are certain characteristics of today's youth culture that are in conflict with the demands of Christian faith.

The Way We Were

Before we examine these characteristics, let us try to understand this latest breed of young Catholics. To do so, it will help to recall a few things about the old breed and the last two new breeds. For purposes of clarity, and at the risk of over-simplification, I will divide them into three groups: the Old Breed of the 1950s, the first New Breed of the 1960s, and the second New Breed which emerged in the 1970s and hasn't changed much since then.

The Old Breed, turned out in the 1950s, is, for all practical purposes, indistinguishable from those of the 1940s, 1930s and 1920s. This group sees God as Creator, Lord and Judge. He is a transcendent deity, all-holy and all-just, who demands and deserves our worship and obedience. To those who fulfill His commands, He dispenses rewards, mostly after death; to those who disregard Him, He threatens punishment, also to take place after death. If you are disobedient in small matters, you go to purgatory, which is quite hot and uncomfortable for a while. If you are very bad and don't get to confession in time, you go to hell, which is very hot and extremely uncomfortable forever.

This is a God you have to take seriously. You'd better not get Him too mad, because He can make it tough for you. Now we know that this wasn't all they told us about God in the 1940s and 1950s; He was also called a God of love, whom we should try to serve out of love and not out of fear. But for many people it was the rewarding-punishing God who came through.

What kind of religious style was generated by this vision of God? At its best, it was a religiousness characterized by reverence, a sense of the sacred, a stress on the virtues of docility and obedience and an abiding sense of sin and of the need for repentance and forgiveness. It often produced genuine heroism and sanctity. At its worst, it produced a static, passive, socially irresponsible, guilt-ridden, minimalistic kind of religion. Static, because it was unable to deal creatively with change. Passive, for it stressed God's power and dominion at the expense of the human person's responsibility and self-determination. This in turn led to social irresponsibility: a failure to confront aggressively those unjust social structures and patterns that religious reactionaries always ignore. (Paradoxically, in areas like sexuality, there was often an exaggerated and unhealthy guilt, expressed in quaint taboos that have helped make George Carlin rich and which still bring a sheepish smile to our faces when we remember those bad old days.) And then there was minimalism, the natural child of legalism and juridicism, which told you how far you could go without committing a mortal sin and sometimes seemed to reduce the Eucharistic celebration to the fulfillment of an obligation.

You can still find all these characteristics alive and well and dozing at many a 10 o'clock Mass; worshipers who come out of a sense of duty, sit passive and inert, are hypersensitive to the most harmless changes in routine, resent exhortations to social justice, are suspicious of those who feel less guilty than they do and come to life only during the race out of the parking lot. They are not bad people, but they have a need to grow, and their vision of God and their religious style do not help move them along.

The religious culture spawned by this vision of God collapsed in the 1960s under the impact of the Second Vatican Council, television, family mobility, the birth control dispute, the civil rights revolution and the Vietnam war. Suddenly authority was out, and conscience was in. Loyalty, stability, commitment were suspect; autonomy, self-fulfillment, "hanging loose" were now approved. Sex was okay, and you could even enjoy it, so long as nobody got hurt. Intellect was deposed in a bloodless coup, and feeling was enthroned. The sacred was out, and secularity was in. Sin was no longer the breaking of rules, but apathy in the face of social evil. God stopped being transcendent and became immanent. Jesus might or might not be divine, but it didn't matter so long as He was really human. Religion ceased to be vertical and became horizontal. We came to church not to find God but to meet and share with one another.

This description, of course, is overdrawn and deliberately so. But can anyone who remembers the 1960s say that none of this happened? That decade of social upheaval witnessed the phenomenon known as throwing out the baby with the bath. It bore witness to the perennial human tendency not only to react to extremes but to overreact. Many good things happened during those years, but some important things were lost, too. We paid a heavy price for evolution that was long overdue.

The inevitable backlash came in the 1970s. The winding down of the war, the end of the civil rights struggle, the easing of polarization within church and society, a shrinking economy, inflation and unemployment brought on a sober reappraisal of our condition. Here was born the back-to-the-basics movement in all kinds of education, including religious education. Unfortunately, with our penchant for overreaction, this took the form not of restoring a sane balance of values, but a reactionary swing to the right. Kids stopped marching for justice and peace and joined the "me" generation. Teachers found them a lot easier to handle, but kind of dull, too. Educational innovation was discredited. Activism was no longer in vogue.

But we were talking about God, weren't we? Well, what happened to God in the 1960s and 1970s? He changed very significantly—not in Himself, of course, but in the minds of those who believe in Him. And the changes have had a profound impact on religious consciousness and style among both old and young, with important implications for religious education and the future of the church.

John Milhaven was one of the first to sight and chart this change. Observing the falling-off in the number of confessions, even by serious and committed Catholics, he ascribed it to a changing sense of sin. The latter coincided with the demise of legalism and juridicism and the rise of personalism in moral theology. At the same time, many adult Catholics were experiencing a metamorphosis not only in their sense of sin but in their vision of God. The rejection of legalism implied the de-emphasis on God as law-giver and judge. Movements like marriage encounter, Cursillo and some charismatic groups, with their strong accent on the acceptance of feelings and emotion in religious expression, encouraged a concept of God not as omnipotent sovereign but as tender lover. This was bound to affect the experience of guilt and the practice of confession. Nor is this the only ambiguity that accompanies this changing vision. On the one hand, it has obviously enriched the church with genuine vitality and enthusiasm. It has encouraged prayer and contemplation and a return to the sources of solid Christian spirituality. On the other, it has loosened the bonds of loyalty to the institutional church and has sometimes encouraged an exaggerated religious individualism.

But if the changing picture of God among adults is varied and ambiguous, it is remarkably homogeneous in its manifestations among the young. I believe that, at this moment in the American Catholic experience, we can state categorically that the great majority of young people see God not as Creator, Lord and Judge, but as Friend, Lover and Companion. Their religious experience is much more horizontal than vertical. Certain expressions occur over and over again. They say they don't like a religion that "puts God on a pedestal"; they don't like to think of Him as almighty sovereign. Their reaction to a film in which Bob Newhart portrays God is nearly always the same: they like Newhart's God because he's so ordinary, so self-effacing, so much "on our level."

Now this is very interesting. These young people seem to have gotten the message, much better than their parents did, that Jesus worked so hard to get across: that His Father is a loving, gentle friend who wants to be called *Abba*—"Daddy." On the other hand, I am uncomfortable with the idea of bringing God *completely* down to my level. I want him "on a pedestal," in some sense, at least. He is the Almighty, the Lord of the Universe, the All-Holy One, the God who is totally other, before whom the angels bow down in reverential awe.

When I hear my students resist this notion of a God who is somehow Our Lord who exercises some kind of dominion over us, I am reminded of the observation made by religious sociologist Will Herberg that most Americans had replaced the God of Moses and Jesus with a deity more to their liking and specifications:

> Religion is expected to produce a kind of spiritual euphoria, the comfortable feeling that one is all right with God. Roy Eckardt calls this the cult of 'divine-human chumminess' to which God is envisioned as the 'Man Upstairs,' a 'Friendly Neighbor,' who is always ready to give you the pat on the back you need when you happen to feel blue. Fellowship with the Lord is, so to say, an extra emotional jag that keeps (us) happy. The 'Gospel' makes (us) 'feel real good.' . . . All sense of the ambiguity and precariousness of human life, all sense of awe before the divine majesty, is shut out. . . . What relation has this kind of God to the biblical God who confronts sinful man as an enemy before He comes out to meet repentant man as a Saviour? Is this He of Whom we are told, 'It is a fearful thing to fall into the hands of the living God'? (Heb. 10-31)[1]

Deja Vu All Over Again

It is more than coincidental that Herberg's observations seem so timely almost four decades later. There are some curious similarities between the religiosity of the 1950s and the 1990s. He characterized the religion of Americans in those days not as belief in a God who had revealed Himself but as a belief in religion itself. It was President Eisenhower who spoke for many of his fellow citizens when he said: "A country like ours makes no sense unless it is founded on some kind of religious belief—*and I don't care what it is* (emphasis added)." One of my students once said almost the same thing to me. I had remarked that the important thing to determine about Christianity was whether it was *true*; and I appealed to the authority of St. Paul who said: "If Christ is not risen from the dead, then we have nothing to preach, and you have nothing to believe" (I Cor. 15:15). My young friend firmly rejected this, and insisted that the important thing is not to believe what's *true*, but to believe in *something*. The next evening, at the parent-teacher meetings, I passed this on to his mother. Far from disagreeing with her son, she backed him 100 per cent, and in no uncertain terms!

Are these people unusual? Well, Rabbi Davis had almost the same conversation with a young man whom he was deprogramming. He said, "What I believed (in the cult) may have been nonsense, (but) at least I was believing. My parents believe nothing." Herberg put it this way:

> It is only too evident that the religiousness characteristic of Americans is very often a religiousness without religion, a religiousness with almost any kind of content or none, a way of sociability or belonging rather than a way of reorienting life to God. It is thus frequently a religiousness without serious commitment, without real inner conviction, without genuine existential decision. What should reach down to the core of existence, shattering and renewing, merely skims the surface of life, and yet succeeds in generating the sincere feeling of being religious. Religion thus becomes a kind of protection the self throws up against the radical demands of faith.[2]

What does all this have to do with Catholic religious education and youth ministry? I think it was John Calvin who said that the human mind is an idol factory in constant operation. In responding to the religious aspirations and longings of American youth today, we have a duty to offer them not just any kind of God or any kind of religion. We are supposed to be faithful to the Gospel that has been entrusted to us. We believe in the God of Moses and Jesus. Jesus knew Him better than Moses did, but He is the same God. He is the Lord of life, and we are the work of his hands, not the other way around. This is not nearly as obvious as it may seem, at least not to the young. It is difficult for many of them even to see that one view of God may be more true than another. The very notion of truth is problematic for them. Doesn't everyone make his or her own truth? Aren't all religions, like value systems and philosophies, just points of view?

This kind of subjectivism is by no means universal among young people, but it occurs quite frequently. To people with this mentality, all assertions about God or Jesus or about moral right or wrong are just that: assertions. Their value lies not in being true but in being agreeable to the one who makes them. And so Christianity becomes not good *news*, but a point of view that is congenial. Jesus is important not because He may be God's Son but because He makes me feel good. And a church is judged not by whether God is worshiped there in Spirit and truth, or whether the Word is faithfully proclaimed and the sacraments duly celebrated. On the contrary, a church is judged by the attractiveness of its ritual, the friendliness of its members and their ability to make me feel at home.

All this is not to be construed as a putdown of the young. Far from it. I have been impressed and heartened by the religious aspirations of many young people I know. Their insights and sensitivity are often strikingly profound and genuinely inspired. But all things human are flawed and imperfect. We should never be surprised when people—even every good people—vindicate Calvin by shaping a God to their own specifications. It is our calling, as ministers of the word, to test the spirit that moves us and our children.

How can we do this? Well, in my case, I did it quite by accident. My junior class was studying the sacrament of reconciliation. I asked them: Why are people confessing less and enjoying it more? Why is the very notion of *sin* out of fashion? One of my most earnest and conscientious students wrote the following: "Man has recreated the role of God from an almighty king to an equal lover. This frees him from the guilt that a view of God as king would entail. This new look drastically cuts down the number of actions man considers serious enough to call a sin. Because this relaxed Christianity fits so well with our life-styles, most people now think of such terms as mortal sin and eternal damnation as archaic and ridiculous. Sin has lost its culpability in the fact that man no longer shapes himself to the demands of Christianity, but that Christianity is now shaped by the needs and whims of man."

Why We're Boring

If this student has not overstated the case, he may have given us an insight into another nagging problem: why so many youngsters complain about church and religion being boring. True, one reason for this may be the fact that we are dealing with a generation raised on television and unable to respond to anything less than constant stimulation. But another possible explanation suggests itself. Most adolescents can put up with boredom provided they are convinced that what they are doing is important. Maybe the kind of God we have communicated and the kind of religion we have produced in the last two decades are dull because, in the last analysis, they don't really seem to matter. If, instead of feeling the need to orient our lives to the wishes of a transcendent and sovereign Creator, we are fashioning a God and a belief system and a set of values to fit our own needs, why should we fear His judgment? When God is reduced completely to our level, and the human person becomes the center of the universe, not only does guilt disappear, but urgency as well.

By contrast, a careful reading of the New Testament shows us Jesus and His followers insistently calling us to conversion and faith. On every page and in a hundred ways they tell us that we are playing for high stakes. Nothing less than our very life, our survival in the deepest sense, hangs in the balance. The Catholicism of the Old Breed, for all its limitations, caught that note and held it. Read the great Catholic novels and even lesser literature that portrayed the church of a few decades ago. There are powerful currents of guilt and fear and hope. One senses that there is wrestling with angels and demons. That kind of religion often labored under real shortcomings that today are painfully evident, but it was never dull. Even at its least inspired, it was clearly about something important. There was a God you had to take seriously. The stakes were high, and you could just as easily lose as win, for the gate was narrow that led to life.

There is no returning to the church or the religion of a bygone time. You can't go home again, even if you want to. But surely there is room for improvement in the way the Christian message is being presented to and perceived by young people in today's church. Any time people greet the good news of Jesus Christ with a yawn, you can be sure they haven't heard it.

I am suggesting we present to young people not just a Jesus who makes me feel good or a God who wants whatever I want, but a God of judgment who challenges human pretensions. This is no idol. Idols always tell us what we want to hear. The God of Moses and Jesus is full of surprises, alternately consoling and discomfiting. He does more than answer our questions; He makes us ask new questions. Over and over, He exposes the illusion of human self-sufficiency.

The God of the Old Breed was something like that, if conceived too narrowly. He was not allowed to surprise us except within carefully drawn limits. Young people who take religion seriously see only too clearly how that kind of religion falls short. They see it in adult congregations in parishes that are turned in on themselves, worried about the wrong things, boring and bored, playing sterile religious games that have no discernible impact for good on themselves or on the world about them. The young don't want to be part of something that looks narrow, uninspiring, cramping, dying or dead. They ascribe this bad scene to the Policeman God of a rulekeeping church taught by moralistic teachers and managed by greedy clerics who preside over dull liturgies. When they ask for bread, this church seems to offer a stone. Well, what do we offer them, bread, or potato chips?

Starting Over

Catechesis in the last years of the twentieth century must build on what is best in the religion of young people and challenge them to aim higher. Assure them that their warm, friendly Lover God is indeed the true God, but that He is also the all-holy, sovereign Creator who is infinitely above us even as He reaches down to share our lot. Show them that the real love of

God and neighbor is more than a vague, warm feeling of benevolence without focus or direction. Tell them that love makes demands; that it costs; that it sometimes hurts. That it leads to a Cross.

When they complain that Mass is boring, tell them it's always been boring! Admit that we (and they) should keep trying to make it more interesting. But break the news to them that the most important things in life are tedious at least part of the time. Education is often boring, but we don't drop out of school, not if we have a brain in our head. Research in science and medicine is humdrum, but it enriches our lives in marvelous ways. A thousand and one jobs are dull but crucial to the functioning and well-being of society. Even meals are sometimes unexciting, but we keep showing up, three times a day, with remarkable fidelity.

When our children say that they prefer to follow their conscience rather than a set of rules, teach them how to form a conscience. And how to examine their conscience before confession; many of them don't have a clue. When they complain about hypocrisy and mediocrity in the church, admit what is true, but help them to see the beam in their own eyes. Tell them that the standard for church teaching is not whether people will find it congenial or comfortable, but whether it measures up to the hard sayings of Jesus Christ. Explain that the church's mission, in any age, is not to invent a message that the many will find reasonable, but to proclaim, in season and out of season, the unadulterated Gospel. When the kids say that the church must change with the times, point out the limits on the truth of that statement.

If, like your students, you don't like a rigid, unyielding, monolithic church, don't trade it in for a bowl of jelly. If you don't like the puritanical, repressive way we used to teach about sex, don't go to the other extreme and give them the impression that anything goes as long as they're sincere and feel good about themselves.

Am I proposing some kind of educational neoconservatism? The last thing I want is a swing to the right in religious education and formation. The very real achievements of the last three decades must not be undervalued or abandoned. There are so many ways in which the religious condition of young Catholics is healthy and hopeful, and these should not be obscured by the limitations and ambiguities pointed out here. We must not return to authoritarianism and indoctrination. We dare not go back on our commitment to education as liberation, especially when reactionaries in the church perceive an opportunity to roll back the gains made in genuine renewal since the council.

What I am asking is that we be humble and self-critical in assessing what has happened to Catholic religious education in the last few decades. In protecting our flank against ignorant and unreasonable critics, let us not be deaf to deserved criticism or blind to our own failings. Much remains to be done if our efforts are to bear the rich fruit of which they are capable.

Can this agenda be addressed? Is it possible for us to achieve the goals I have set out for faithful and effective religious formation of the young? Yes, but on condition that we, the elders, take these things to heart and put our own house in order. We cannot give what we do not have. Young people in the church cannot develop a faith and a viable religious culture if adults do not show the way. If we are divided or timid or confused or weak, the kind of renewal I am urging can hardly take place.

We have to work to educate a generation of Catholics who will meet the challenge of faith better than we did. Could we turn out Catholics who would not be so easy to stereotype? People with real values and character and loyalties, but capable of critical thinking, with healthy attitudes toward authority, who would help bail out the Barque of Peter but who would try to make the helmsman shape up?

Let's Aim High

For catechesis in the rest of this century and beyond, I suggest the following goals. Let us present the good news of Jesus Christ in such a way that, as far as we can, we produce young people who are successful, but not just consumers; who are industrious and hardworking, but also compassionate toward the poor; people of strong character who can have pity on the weak; who are against premarital sex but are not puritanical; who are not only against abortion, but who also have reservations about warmaking and capital punishment; who are patriotic without being jingoistic; who are capable of loyalty to institutions but are critical people of conscience; who accept the guidance of the church but are willing to take responsibility for their lives; who are well instructed in their religion but are open to new ideas and perspectives; who know how to be committed without being rigid; who can worship a God of majesty and power yet be on intimate terms of tenderness with Him; who have a healthy sense of self-worth and yet can acknowledge their sinfulness; who can hate sin but love sinners; who can love even the people they don't like.

These are lofty goals indeed. But Catholic schools are supposed to aim high. We are not turning out, in great numbers, Catholic graduates like the ones I have just described. But we can try. Just making the effort will bring our schools closer to the ideal of being schools with a difference. Different not only from non-Catholic schools, but different from what we used to be, and different from what we are. We have come a long way from the Old Breed of thirty years ago. In those thirty years many good things have happened, and many not so good. To turn out a New Breed for the twenty-first century that will give life and hope to the church and the world, we still have a long way to go.

Topics for Discussion

1. Has your image of God changed over the years? How?

2. How have the changes in religious images and styles during the last few decades affected you and your religious practise?

3. Do you think that young people can relate to a God who is at once consoling and demanding?

Notes

1. *Protestant, Catholic, Jew,* Doubleday, 1957, p. 266.
2. *Ibid.* p. 260.

Chapter 3

Will My Child Keep the Faith?

ON ONE THING NEARLY ALL CATHOLICS AGREE: IT'S HARDER THAN ever to bring up children Catholic. If you are the parent of older children, you probably know from experience that passing on your religious faith is no easy matter. Their belief in Christian doctrine, their ideas of right and wrong, and their attitudes toward Church membership and attendance may clash with your own convictions and cause you understandable anxiety.

If you have the impression that it is more difficult for you to share your faith than it was for your parents, you're absolutely right. This is true not only because young people are different from what they used to be, but because adults have changed as well. Although there are still many whose way of thinking and feeling and being Catholic hasn't changed in the past 30 years, this unchanged group is outnumbered by those who have grown up or matured in a very different kind of Church.

Among the new breed of adults, attitudes toward authority, sin, prayer and celebration are significantly different. And since children pick things up by watching grown-ups, their own religious and moral style is bound to be affected. What is disconcerting and even frightening to many of the adults who welcomed the reforms of the Second Vatican Council and considered them enriching for their own lives and the life of the Church is that their children are not impressed but rather bored and alienated.

Of course, we know that people, even young people, cannot be "programmed" for Christian belief and practice. Faith is ultimately a free response to God's grace, and no one can be forced into it. Even in the "good old days" we had our share of religious dropouts. But the problem is undeniably bigger today, and it often starts sooner.

So it's reasonable to ask: Are there any reliable indicators of my son's or daughter's progress in Christian faith and values? Is there anything I can do to help? Yes, there are, and you can. But first, a few words about faith itself.

Faith Is a Process

When we worry about people not keeping the faith, we think of them as "losing" it. This is a fair description of what happens to some adults. People in their mature years can and do revise their beliefs, change values, abandon old commitments and make new ones. With respect to children and young people, however, the abandoning of religious practice or Church membership rarely represents a conscious decision to change the direction of one's life. More than likely, what has happened is a failure to grow.

Faith, after all, is not a *thing;* it is a *relationship* with God and his people. Relationships don't get kept or lost exactly; they either grow or stagnate and die. Sometimes they don't even get off the ground. We all get introduced to countless people in our lifetime; with some we become acquaintances, with others, lifelong friends. And still others remain strangers. Relationships are born of encounters and deepen with sharing and communication. Some of our deepest loyalties begin in childhood and ripen throughout life; but most childhood friendships fail to survive our growing up. We do not reject these persons; we simply grow away from them as we move or change or enlarge our world.

Do we "give" faith to an infant at baptism? Yes and no. Yes, the child encounters Christ within the Church and receives a share in God's life. Something real happens at baptism. But it is not magic. It is the beginning of something beautiful, but only a beginning. It is as fragile and unpredictable as newborn infants themselves. It must be nourished by example and education and discipline, like all the other good things that parents want to share with their child.

Don't think of faith as a finished thing which we receive early in life and are admonished not to lose. Rather, it is like a seed that starts small and can grow into a giant tree, provided the tender plant receives water and sunlight and protection from blight.

Faith Is Free

The first steps in religious formation—teaching prayers, telling Bible stories, early instruction in doctrine—are, in a way, imposed on the child. All the choices are made for them by parents and other adults. But before long, youngsters learn that other people do not believe or value what their parents believe and value. By adolescence, they realize that other choices are open to them. Moreover, many other influences in their young lives are enticing and pressuring them to choose paths different from the ones marked out at home.

Some young people will never consciously choose; they will just drift. The world is full of people who have never freely chosen their way of life but simply respond to social pressures. Some Church people are like that, but not as many as there used to be.

More and more people, as they grow up, realize that being born into a Church community and raised according to its teachings is not enough reason for an adult to accept those teachings without question. For some, the questioning begins quite early, during high school or even junior high years.

This is how one high school senior put it:

> The youth of today are more independent, more self-reliant than ever before. They question everything they meet. They are less willing to accept doctrines and judgments as being right without first examining them and judging them on personal experience. . . . Young people are no longer content to accept the religion of their parents and teachers . . . simply because it is the religion of these people and the religion they are taught when young.

> Instead of quiet acceptance, there is . . . a point or period of crisis during which the individual realizes he must choose either to accept or to reject the faith before him. The consequences of this decision are so great that, I believe, many young people do not really make a definite choice without hesitation or doubt for several years.

And the choice is not a one-shot thing. It must be made again and again, as people pass from youth to young adulthood to maturity and on to middle age and beyond.

Eight Ways to Assist Your Child's Faith-Development

Will your child choose to be Catholic? To the extent that he or she accomplishes the following eight tasks of personal development, there is a good chance that the answer will be yes. It is important, therefore, that we help our youth to:

1. *Achieve Religious Literacy.* We cannot love or choose what we do not know. If we have little or no idea what Christianity is, or what our Church teaches, we will be unable to make an intelligent choice for or against religious commitment. Religious instruction, first at home and then in school or parish program, is a crucial element in the formation of a religious identity.

Feeling good about ourselves and being sensitive to the rights and needs of others are very important, but these qualities do not of themselves make us Christians. The gospel is more than a call to humanism; it is a unique vision of God and the world and ourselves. Contrary to popular mythology, all religions are *not* the same, and they are not equal.

"Teaching kids their religion," of course, is not so easy. Christianity is an adult faith, a grown-up's way of relating to life, and it loses a lot in translation for the young. That's why Jesus didn't formally try to teach children, except, of course, by his example and loving attitudes. There are legitimate differences among catechetical theorists about how religious instruction should be given. The ideal lies somewhere between the extremes of the Baltimore Catechism and the "balloon books." The former tries to teach too much too soon, the latter shortchange the children by reducing religious concerns to vague exhortations to benevolence.

If we're not very clear about the difference, then maybe we should be concerned not only about our children but about our own level of religious literacy. When did we have our last serious religious thought or learning experience?

2. Learn Religious Skills. In order to feel at home in a religious setting, one must know how to act and what to do. Children need to be taught how to pray and how to celebrate. They should master ritual gestures and formulas, first by memorization, later in more reflective and sophisticated ways. Adolescents usually reject rote recitation; they should be taught various forms of prayer that are less structured, more individual and spontaneous. But as younger children they need more structure than some of them are getting. First teach them prayers, then teach them *how* to pray.

Do your teenagers, for example, know how to participate in the Sacrament of Reconciliation? There have been many changes in the rite, and their style of "confession" may be quite different from yours; no problem. But do they know how to examine their conscience? Can they tell the difference between this sacrament and a friendly chat? Do they know what to say or do?

3. *Discover Experiences of Community.* If a young person is to grow up comfortable with Church, he or she must have some good experiences of doing religious things together with others. Everyone understands and accepts the fact that Church cannot always be interesting or exciting. Even children can tolerate a certain amount of boredom. But if experiences of worship and common prayer are *always* dull and unimaginative, and if liturgical celebrations are *never* touched by warmth and a sense of group involvement, can we blame youngsters for trying to avoid such experiences? Some parish congregations are consistently passive and unresponsive. Some priests are always tiresome and uninspired. If all the TV shows were this bad, kids would give up watching the tube.

4. *Try to Live Like a Christian.* Some people stop going to church because they're living in a way that makes them uncomfortable there. Young people who deal in drugs, dishonesty or sexual promiscuity feel like hypocrites in Christian assemblies, and in a way they're right.

On a less spectacular but no less serious level, some are so completely self-absorbed that they cannot respond to calls to unselfish concern for others. Jesus came to call sinners, but they had to be at least open to a better way of life. True, we said above that feeling good about yourself and being sensitive to others does not make you a Christian, but they are a necessary foundation. Grace builds on nature.

5. *Ask Religious Questions.* Christianity is more than a vague summons to acknowledge God's existence and be nice to others. It is the answer to the deepest questions one can ask about human existence. We can encourage our children to ask such questions: Are we alone in the universe, or is there a God who watches over us? Does life have any transcendent purpose? Are we mere accidents of evolution, or part of a plan that includes an eternal destiny? What is the strongest force in the universe—death or life? What does it mean to be a good human being?

These are the questions Jesus came to answer. They are adult questions, but youths and even children ask them sometimes. In a culture as shallow and superficial as ours, some need help to ask such questions. If you never put such questions with personal urgency, then churchgoing cannot be anything more for you than a formalistic response to social pressure. Such conventional religiosity is dying out. From now on, religion must be made of sterner stuff.

6. *Ask for the Giant Size.* Christianity not only is the answer to life's most fundamental questions, but also promises the fulfillment of the deepest longings of the human heart. All of us have a desire for health, for security, for friendship, for life. Doctors, bankers and insurance companies can help us with these, but not the way Jesus does. Some people lose interest in religion not because they want too much but because they want too little.

In the world in which our children grow up, it is possible to settle for a very limited vision of what we can expect out of life. A foreign observer once noted that, for many Americans, heaven would be an infinitely large department store with an unlimited supply of gadgets, trinkets and baubles. Andrew Greeley says that the Good News is too good for most people to believe. Their problem is not just closed minds but also closed hearts. To come to faith, you have to ask for the giant size.

7. *Grow Up With Serious Religious People.* Good parental example doesn't guarantee that young people will grow up Catholic, but it's an almost universally necessary precondition. This is no news to anyone; we always knew that parents played a crucial role in a child's faith development.

What is news is that a somewhat different kind of example is required today. No longer is it enough to teach children prayers, send them to religious instruction, go with them to Sunday Mass and "keep the rules" for the rest of the week. Twenty years ago that formula turned out conventional Catholics with remarkable regularity. But, as we pointed out above, conventional religiosity doesn't make it any more. Young people find it hard to take it seriously, for it doesn't make a more than superficial impact on the way people live. "Hypocrites" is the harsh word they use for people who are strict on Church attendance, offensive language and sexual taboos, and permissive about dishonesty, bigotry and social apathy.

This is not to say that parents have to be saints. Most of us are just sinners doing the best we can. But growing children need to see that their parents' religious affiliation and Church membership has some discernible effect on their values and life-style Teenagers get depressed and even cynical about the yawning gap between what people say inside church and what they do outside it.

It helps when they know that their parents, in accordance with their Catholic profession, are at least *trying* to be better. If you were accused of being a Christian, could they find enough evidence to convict you? Or put it this way: Does your religion give you resources for living, for dealing with life's ups and downs? Does it ever push you to try to do more than "love God and keep the rules and not hurt anybody"?

Outside of Sunday Mass, what do you give in the way of time, energy and talent to your Church and its activities? Your kids are probably not terribly impressed by your regularity and rule-keeping. But if your style of being Catholic includes generosity, openness and involvement, they can at least take you and your religion seriously.

8. See Faith as a Call to Maturity. As young people grow up, they turn away from the things of childhood. A child's view of religious realities like God, Church, faith, sin and forgiveness is inadequate for the adolescent and the young adult. Presentations of religion that stress exclusively the childhood virtues of obedience, dependence and docility can create the impression that God and Church don't want us to grow up—that they are less comfortable with us when we reach out for the independence, self-reliance and responsibility that go with adulthood.

Adolescents must hear that our Church stands not only for authority but also for the rights of personal conscience. We must show them that a developing capacity for critical thought, far from threatening their faith, is a desirable asset for the thinking, grown-up Catholic. Most young adults want to be asked by their Church to do more than pray, pay and obey.

Teenagers have a name for the kind of passive piety that still appeals to many older people. They call it a security blanket. If we want them to keep the faith, we have to present it as something they are to continually aspire to, not something they will outgrow.

Today's Youth Are Hungry

Don't get the idea, from all that we have said, that young people are hostile to religious faith. They are resisting certain *ways* of being religious, but not religion itself. The fact that particular expressions and styles of belief turn them off does not mean that they have given up the search for faith. The vast majority of teenagers are hungry for something or someone to believe in. Even as they shy away in fear from long-term commitments, they yearn for values or causes that might deserve their loyalty.

The popularity of fundamentalist groups and the phenomenon of cults are striking evidence of this hunger for direction and larger meaning. Even though such cults attract only a minority, it is significant that those involved are often among the most sensitive and idealistic members of a generation that often seems rootless and confused.

Our children are restless. Many long for a fuller life than our times seem to offer them. Jesus said that he came that we might have life and have it more abundantly. Unlike cult leaders, he gives no easy answers. Unlike advertisers and other media manipulators, he promises no quick fix or instant gratification. He offers only the paradoxical pledge that on the other side of sacrifice, unselfishness, integrity and generosity lies the fullness of life.

This is the kind of vision that has never lost the power to win minds and hearts. It can captivate our children, too, but only if it is presented not as a narrow, constricting ideology but as a *call to greatness*. And that call must be expressed not only in words but in deeds, in living people as close to them as you and me.

Topics for Discussion

1. What were the experiences that you remember from your childhood and adolescence, that had a positive or negative impact on your religious development?

2. What does religion mean to you besides "love God and keep the rules and don't hurt anybody"?

3. What do you think of young people's criticism and rejection of adult religious practise? Is it honest, or just a rationalization of their own shortcomings?

Chapter 4

The Religious Needs of Teens

WATCH ANY GROUP OF PEOPLE, YOUNG OR OLD, AS THEY WORSHIP and pray together, and you can be sure that the quality of their celebration will depend largely on three factors: their vision of God, their sense of themselves, and their experience of community. When the congregation is homogeneous in its make-up, and confined to one age-span or ethnic or social grouping, their religious style will be fairly predictable.

Fervor and enthusiasm, the hallmarks of a "successful" liturgy, are influenced by many other variables such as planning, setting, and leadership skills. But even these depend on the way the worshipers think and feel about God, themselves, and one another.

Consider how these observations are verified in some adult liturgies. As you may have noticed, many parish churches which have three or four Sunday Masses find that each celebration takes on a predictable coloration. A case in point is a parish where I recently preached at all three Sunday Masses. The pastor predicted, accurately, that the 8:00 a.m. group would be very quiet and reserved; that the 10:00 a.m. congregation would be lively and receptive; and that the folks at the 12:15 would get restless if they didn't make the parking lot by one o'clock!

Take the 8:00 a.m. crowd. They are older people, reverent but reserved, polite but not demonstrative. Theirs is a very "vertical" kind of piety. God, to most of them is perceived as a Supreme Being, a Lawgiver and Judge, who rewards the good and punishes the wicked. They see this Eucharist primarily as the fulfillment of an obligation under pain of serious sin. They are a fairly conventional group, keenly attuned to the demands of propriety, especially the maintaining of a hushed silence. Jokes from the pulpit, even good ones, are guaranteed to fall flat; better save them for the 10 o'clock Mass. The handshake of peace is awkward and constrained. There is little sense of community, since these people, for most of their lives, have thought of the Eucharist not as a group sharing of faith, but as the individual fulfillment of a religious duty. The level of personal interaction is low, for the simple reason that it is not a felt need, not expected, and not even desirable.

The scene described is worlds removed from a teenage "folk" Mass. These young people have a much more "horizontal" religious style. They like to think of God not as a lawgiver or judge, but as a friend and companion. In theological terms, their God is seen as immanent rather than transcendent. At an age when they are rearranging their relationships with parents and parent surrogates, and resent adults who call for obedience and docility, an authority-figure God is perceived as threatening and hence rejected or denied. But a God who is a friend, who accepts them, who is "on their level," is attractive to them. Religion then, becomes less a matter of reverence and mystery and more a matter of friendship and intimacy. The Eucharist is valued not as an opportunity to fulfill an obligation or to get a reward or to escape a punishment, but as a chance to experience warmth and acceptance.

These attitudes come through rather clearly in a teenage boy's written comments on two liturgies he attended:

Today's was a typical Mass which I would give a rating of 4 on a scale of 10 (10 being the best). The rituals were performed and the priest gave his sermon. He told the congregation that we are Jesus' helpers. I disagree with this because I think of Jesus more as a partner and not as a slave master. My church consistently preaches God as our master instead of our friend. I disagree with this because you cannot have a close friendship between two people, if one of the two is constantly being placed on a pedestal. . . .

We have a summer house in New Jersey, and the church there is modern and has two fairly young and energetic priests. I rate their Masses a "9+" *because there is feeling of togetherness and brotherhood. The Church must practice more peace and brotherhood if it wishes to survive.*

Not only one's vision of God, but also one's self-concept directly affects religious expectations and style. Young adolescents are persons who, a few short years ago, were still children and lived in a child's world, where the important thing was to fulfill adult expectations and gain adult approval. That was a very "vertical" world, where "big people" made the rules and set the tone for most serious activities, including church. As little kids, they got bored and squirmed and misbehaved, but they were too helpless and dependent to rebel. But now, in the junior high years, the "significant others" are not just their parents but also their peers. Status, identity, and relationships are undergoing revision. They are no longer sure of who they are or of what is expected of them. They want desperately to be accepted and to belong.

If religion and religious activities respond to and fulfill these needs, they are esteemed; otherwise, they are likely lo be disvalued or rejected.

Learning by Experience

This was brought home to me one morning when I presided at Eucharist in the high school where I teach. In the chapel were several of my students. During and immediately after the liturgy, I felt happy with the way it had gone: the level of participation had seemed encouraging; my homily, I thought, had been effective and to the point. As always, I had tried to be warm and outgoing, so that I might involve the boys in the celebration.

So I was feeling moderately pleased with myself when, later in the morning, I casually asked for their reaction to the service. To my surprise, they politely but firmly informed me that they didn't like it at all! I tried to avoid being defensive; instead, I asked them to explain what I had done wrong. Their replies, I believe, can give us some insight into the religious world of the young—a world often markedly different from that of their elders.

What were their objections? Although they never used the word, their complaints indicated that my style of celebration was too *vertical*. They contrasted my church manners with my classroom style, which is informal, relaxed, egalitarian. When trying to be reverent and prayerful, I came across as stiff and aloof. My homily was criticized as being authoritarian and judgmental; to this day, I have no idea what they were talking about.

Part of the problem seems to have been my change of roles, from discussion leader to religious celebrant. But this tells us nothing about adolescents and religion, only that they like their adults predictable. The "worship gap" that showed up between me and my students went much further than that. It came, I believe, from a way of picturing and thinking about God and our relation to him, and a whole set of religious presuppositions and expectations that often set off the young from the old.

When seriously religious adults pray or worship, they try consciously to make contact with Someone greater than themselves. They perceive this Someone as all-holy, majestic, powerful—a loving creator who watches over us and hears us. They try to create a certain "space" for this religious activity through silence and an attitude of reverent listening. Bodily gestures— kneeling, bowing one's head, folding one's hands—all contribute to this reverent atmosphere which is considered appropriate when entering the realm of the sacred. Taken together, these attitudes and gestures constitute the vertical dimension of religious activity and experience: they are our way of relating to God as *transcendent.*

Of course, God is not only transcendent. He is also *immanent.* He not only stands over and above reality, but is at the very heart of it. He is Other, but he is also within us. And since he is incarnate in Jesus Christ, he is not only infinitely above us but also, paradoxically, on our level. Hence, authentic Christian experience will also have about it an element of the *horizontal.* We truly meet the Lord in one another. Communal prayer and worship are at their best when they manage to combine these elements of reverent attentiveness to God and responsiveness to one another.

Young people today place great value on the horizontal, communal dimensions of religion. For most of them, church should either bring people together in love or be rejected as worthless. The same goes for liturgical worship: if young people do not experience warmth and friendliness, they reject it. Informality and spontaneity are esteemed to the point that the two generations are placed in conflict. Casual behavior in church, which young people consider to be merely relaxed, strikes their elders as irreverent, even blasphemous.

Both groups, I think, are partly right and partly wrong. Adults are sometimes too straitlaced in church; religion does not have to be grim and humorless. Their children are reminding them that God's house can be a joyful, happy place where his sons and daughters can truly feel at home. On the other hand, young people can be so intent on relating to one another that they lose sight of the One who calls all people together. Religious gatherings that are exclusively horizontal become mere love-ins with little or no genuinely religious dimension.

Much of this tension, of course, is due simply to the natural exuberance and gregariousness of the young. They have so much energy—it is not easy for them to achieve the serenity and repose needed for serious prayer. Moreover, praying is like any other skill: It has to be taught and learned. Most youngsters have had little practice, and some have no one to teach them. Besides, it should not be surprising that adolescents and young adults, at an age when they are intensely interested in relationships, should be tempted to reduce religion to an exercise in making friends. As long as adults are patient and understanding, they can help their growing children to develop a spirituality that is authentically Christian.

Not all the difficulties, however, arise from simple youthful high spirits. Today's younger generation is growing up in a milieu that poses peculiar problems for religious growth. I am not referring to the materialism and hedonism of the dominant culture, which are obvious and directly confront religious commitment. No, there are more subtle difficulties arising from within religion itself.

Young people insist, quite rightly, that religion should make a difference in the way people live and treat one another. They are impatient with religious formalism of all kinds: "Sunday morning religion" has a bad reputation among them. Prayer and worship which have no discernible impact on people's values and life-styles strike them as sheer hypocrisy. (By the way, if you're sixteen years old and don't want to get up on Sunday morning, these provide wonderful rationalizations for staying in bed!) It is, then, easy to conclude that religion which "does nothing for me" is worthless. If I "don't get anything" out of Sunday worship, why should I go? If the Christian community in my church is less than ideal, why should I let them infect me with their mediocrity?

Even when the reactions of young people to church and religion are positive, some troubling questions remain. Ask some of the religiously enthusiastic teens what appeals to them, and their replies will be something like this: "Jesus makes me feel good." "Meditation relaxes me." "We have very friendly liturgies." These are not bad reasons, but they are somewhat limited. They reveal a religious motivation which is very subjective and can become quite self-centered. In this kind of religion (which is by no means limited to the young), the center is occupied not by God but by the self. Christianity is valued not because it is true but because it is appealing. A church is chosen not because God is worshiped there in spirit and in truth, but because I find its rituals congenial. The proclamation of the word of God and ritual celebration are of little worth if I don't find them interesting.

Young people need to be encouraged, but they also need to be challenged. They have to be told that love is indeed at the heart of religion, but that it's more than a feeling and it leads to a cross. They must be introduced to a God who does not always tell us what we want to hear. We must gently but firmly insist that the test of a religion is not whether it *appeals to* me, but whether it is true. My job is not to find a god with whom I can be comfortable, but to seek God as he really is. Otherwise, religion degenerates into idolatry. It is very difficult for many people, both young and old, to accept this point of view. The underside of American religious tolerance and pluralism is the unspoken but deeply ingrained feeling that in matters of religion, truth is of no concern. As American as apple pie is the conviction that you can buy the wrong car or take the wrong courses or marry the wrong person, but you can't pick the wrong religion.

Young people are open to religion today; they are searching for something to believe in. They are tired of freedom without direction. They sense the emptiness of hedonism and materialism, and long for something better. This has caused a religious revival of sorts, one which has great possibilities but labors under many handicaps, as I have tried to show. How can the obstacles be surmounted and the possibilities realized?

Wanted: Adult Models

The greatest need that young people have is an adult church community that is alive and well and serious about religion. By "serious" I do not mean grim. Grown-ups must lead the way in conviction and commitment to something larger than themselves, to a vision of reality that transforms one's life for the better. Normally, teenagers cannot be expected to have deep personal convictions and commitments, not at a time of life when they are still finding out who they are and what they stand for.

What they require of adults is not indoctrination or pressure or criticism, but modeling. Even as our growing children seek their identities and ask for elbow room, they want us to be people who know who we are and what we believe. They want to be confident that we are genuinely trying to practice what we preach. This sounds like just plain old-fashioned good example, but it is of a particular kind. It isn't holding our noses and taking our religion like medicine and telling the kids they can do it, too. It means being demonstrably better people because of our religious beliefs—not just strict on church attendance and sex, but also more hopeful, more compassionate, less selfish, more open to life. If religion doesn't do that for us, then the youngsters may rightly ask: "What's so important about it?" This challenges adults to put their money where their mouth is. Mere social or cultural religiosity attracts fewer and fewer young buyers. Faith, if it is to be passed on, must henceforth be made of stronger stuff.

Besides needing adults, young people need one another. One of the most significant and positive developments in youth work of the past decade is the youth-to-youth phenomenon, wherein teens and college students minister to one another. For instance, in certain kinds of popular youth retreats, the talks are given not by clergy or other adults but by peers. Students who have made these retreats become teen members who guide the next group through the experience, while adults stay in the background. The strategy works with impressive frequency, and amounts to a successful end run around the generation gap. In neighborhoods and on college campuses, young Christians who are swimming against a tide of secularism emanating from a hostile dominant culture find affirmation and support in their church youth groups. They play together, they pray together, they make friends and work at building community, while friendly adults provide structure and offer encouragement from the wings.

No matter how effectively youth ministers to youth, adults will be needed to provide for continuity with and fidelity to tradition. This is not the same as trying to make our children copies of ourselves. It means letting them be themselves and helping them to live the Good News in their own distinctive way. Jesus assures us that in our Father's house there are many mansions. The task of Christian parents and teachers and ministers is to let young people find their own mansions, while we help them stay within the household of the faith.

Topics for Discussion

1. Are the vertical and horizontal dimensions of worship important values to you? Does your parish liturgy do justice to both?

2. Do you think the young people of your acquaintance are looking for the right things in worship and prayer?

3. Have you observed peer ministry in action? How effective has it been?

Chapter 5

Evangelizing the Young

THE FUTURE BELONGS TO THE YOUNG. THIS IS AS TRUE FOR CHURCHES and synagogues as it is for nations and other societies. So when the process of socialization shows an unusually high rate of failure, the vitality and even the future of a faith community is threatened. Book titles like *Where Have All The Young People Gone?* and *Will Our Children Have Faith?* reflect adult anxiety over the alienation of adolescents and young adults from organized religion.

The yawning rows of empty pews in once-crowded churches were not all occupied, in better times, by the young. Adults have contributed their share of dropouts in the exodus of Catholics from the post-Vatican II Catholic Church. But the absence of young people in such large numbers is a legitimate cause for alarm among those who care about the survival and the vitality of the church. This concern accounts for a phenomenon quite familiar to many pastors and religious education coordinators who have tried seriously to introduce adult religious learning programs into their parishes. They often find that the only topic likely to bring out the adults is a discussion of "youth and religion"—their moral development, their growth in faith, the causes and cures of their religious estrangement.

This child-centeredness is a fundamental weakness of American religiosity, and will have to be dealt with in its turn. Meanwhile, however, while we bemoan the inability of many older churchgoers to take as active a concern in their own religious development as in that of their children, we do well to take special pains to improve lines of communication with teens and young adults. But, as we shall see, reaching out to young church members will probably have limited success if we do not, at the same time, upgrade the quality of adult religious experience and practice.

Of course, the religious receptivity of adolescents is tied closely to childhood religious experiences and to attitudes and practices within the family circle. The religious nurture of young children has always been a task calling for genuine parental faith and sensitivity to stages of growth. And, as Dolores Curran has pointed out, the good old days are gone, when we could count on the proven formula:

Catholic marriage + parochial school + weekly Mass = good Catholic children.

Even when families do more than this, and provide the kind of effective religious nurture that helps youngsters achieve a religious identity in keeping with their years, important tasks remain in middle and later adolescence. The thrust toward autonomy and independence that characterizes these years poses serious challenges to faith. Young adults must find out not merely what their parents believe and value, but what they themselves accept and prize. In terms proper to Dr. James Fowler's stage theory of faith development, it is time to move from an uncritical, or synthetic-conventional level toward an autonomous or independent-reflexive stage.

Religious educators who deal with this age group find its members very challenging and often frustrating. The reasons for the difficulty are many, but one which I shall develop at some

length is the fact that teachers in school programs and confraternity classes are usually equipped for catechesis and theology but not for the more fundamental approach called evangelization. The distinctions are crucial. Catechesis is the process
of communicating the mysteries and explaining the doctrines and
practices of the Christian faith. Theology is traditionally defined
as "faith seeking understanding"—an intellectual exercise that
aims at deeper comprehension of what is believed and taught.
But, as the new *National Catechetical Directory* (*Sharing the Light of
Faith*) reminds us:

> Catechesis presupposes prior preevangelization and
> evangelization. These are likely to be most successful when
> they build on basic human needs—for security, affection,
> acceptance, growth and intellectual development—show-
> ing how these include a need, a hunger, for God and His
> Word (n. 34).

This process of evangelization, addressing itself to such
"basic human needs," calls for skills that are in short supply
among those of us who share in the ministry of the Word. Most
of us are trained to communicate with active church members, to
elaborate and develop and explain and to give an account of our
faith to those outside the fold. But what of those within the fold
who are uncertain of their commitment and are reexamining
their options? What of those who question not the truth of Christianity but the relevance of the religious quest itself? Hundreds
of times, in my years of teaching religion to Catholic high school
students, I have been asked: "Why is it so important to be a
Catholic? Why do I have to belong to *any* church? Why not just
be a good person?" And for every student who asked these questions, there were many more too disaffected or too bored even to
put them into words.

Even for those who are not negatively disposed, these are
normal questions for young people on the threshold of adulthood. If we agree that the unexamined life is not worth living,
we should welcome probing queries like these, especially when
they arise from a genuine desire for enlightenment.

End of an Era

Before you try to answer, you must understand the source of these questions that were not often asked by youngsters in Catholic instruction programs 30 years ago. John Walsh, a Maryknoll missionary priest, calls it the beginning of the end of cultural Christianity. In his years on the Japanese mission, Father Walsh, working in a non-Christian environment, found that before his neophytes came to conversion and baptism, they had to go through a long personal odyssey of search and discovery. The religious quest, for these converts, is an intensely personal journey that often begins with anxiety or emptiness, is marked by ambivalence and reluctance, passes through confusion and doubt and finally arrives at enlightenment, surrender to grace and commitment. For them, baptism is not an inevitable formality associated with infancy, but an eminently free, adult decision.

Until very recently, Catholics and other Christians born in environments like ours were apparently exempt from such a conversion process. It was enough to be born of Catholic parents, hear religious stories and learn prayers within the family, receive instruction and sacramental preparation in church schools or parish confraternity classes, worship regularly and avail oneself of the church's sacramental ministry. This is the formula described by Dolores Curran. It wasn't foolproof, but it worked with remarkable frequency.

This recently defunct religious culture, at its best, was marked by vitality and strength. It helped produce people of solid piety, genuine commitment and real holiness. Of course, it had its weaknesses, too. It turned out a goodly number of adherents who were Christian by custom and habit, not by conviction or choice. Some of these cultural Christians dropped out or lived on the fringes of the faith community, but many were carried along for a lifetime on a wave of religious conformity that may have lacked depth and sometimes lapsed into formalism but which rather rarely (by today's standards) took the form of explicit estrangement.

We don't need missionaries to tell us that those days are gone forever. But Father Walsh offers more than diagnosis. He prescribes a remedy for the patient and calls it evangelization. By this he does not mean the Bible-quoting, pulpit-thumping kind of pious harangue that many Catholics associate with the term. Rather, he bids us come to terms with the fact that the surrounding culture no longer supports church affiliation and practice. Custom and habit are no longer enough; religious identity, from now on, must be made of sterner stuff. It must be born of personal conviction and free choice.

Baptized Catholics in so-called Christian environments will, more and more, have to go through the search and discovery experiences that precede conversion in places like Japan. This means a new style of religious education and formation, geared not to the preservation of a religious ghetto but to preparing people to function as believers in a pluralistic environment that rarely supports and often discourages religious commitment.

The process is appropriate for adults as well as for youth. This is not surprising, as we have become accustomed to hearing young people ask the kind of adult religious questions that were once reserved to their elders. Many adolescents, by the age of 16 or 17, need not only the answers to religious questions but assistance in asking the questions. As with a large number of their elders, their complaints about church have much deeper roots than mere ecclesial misunderstandings and malfunctions. Sometimes they suffer not only from religious illiteracy but from an almost total lack of authentic religious experience—an absence of prayer, a missing sense of the sacred. Sometimes their ailment is a constriction of the heart or a narrowing of the horizons.

Before God or Jesus or church can be anything more than a bore, you have to be looking for something more out of life than what Sony, Cadillac, Chase Manhattan and even All-State can offer. Even if you have set your sights higher than this, and want to be a "good person," as long as you think you can achieve this alone and unaided, it seems that God is unnecessary, Jesus is superfluous and church is a nuisance. What you need is not religious information but an expansion of your heart's wishes, so that you may ask the questions Christ came to answer and long for the things He came to give. In a word you must be open to the transcendent, hungry for the fullness of life.

For older adolescents, the way to such questioning and seeking is best found through human relationships. Just recently emerged from the narcissism of childhood, they have a hunger for friendship that goes beyond mere acceptance. The possibilities, the demands, the dangers of love fascinate and attract them. They are ready now for a God who is more than an authority figure more than a heteronomous deity meting out capricious rewards and punishments and arbitrarily complicating their existence. They can be introduced to a lover-God who does not force Himself on them but offers friendship with no strings attached except the condition that they love one another. This is precisely the kind of God revealed by Jesus Christ. The latter can now be presented and seen by them not as a superman or a miracle machine or a fuzzy humanist spouting harmless pieties, but as one who calls to integrity in relationships, to the maturity that is possible only to those who are truly open to others.

Even when these connections have been made, much remains to be done. Young adults who are taking this second look at their religious tradition must see it whole before they see it in detail. We must tell them that the faith community that has nurtured them thus far, and that now invites them to free, adult membership, is more than a group of pious people who share humanist ideals. We are more than a movement, we are a church, sharing a faith that makes demands beyond the ordinary and holds out the promise of a life stronger than death. We believe we are an organism, the very Body of Christ, with no less a vital principle than His Holy Spirit.

To help us live up to His values, to which we are committed, we have not only our own strength of character—which is never enough—but also a sacramental system that offers, among other things, the very Bread of Life to be our food. This is why we are not bored by Mass and can cope with less than perfect celebration. This is why we have no doubt that we "are getting something out of it" even when preaching or singing or participation fall short. We are part of something supremely important, that speaks to a part of ourselves that will die if it is neglected. We adult Christians, who belong not by custom or habit but by conviction and choice, go to church not out of fear or conformity but to find a life available nowhere else.

Questions Before Answers

There's a lot more, but you get the idea. This is what we call "getting back to basics"—not grinding out answers to questions our growing children have not yet asked, but helping them to ask the questions, to expand their horizons, to break out of a world too narrow for anything more than self-indulgence and closed to authentic religious vision and experience. Evangelization is more than an attack on religious illiteracy; it is an attempt to dig the only foundations that can support religious commitment in today's world. Teen-agers and young adults, as well as mature persons, can hear a message like this if it comes from Christians who care for them, who respect their stumbling attempts at freedom and leave them a little space even as they try to share a vision. It is a message not for children but for grownups and for those on the threshold of growing up. It is not a sentimental exercise in mindless optimism. It appeals neither to fear nor to conformity. It is straight talk about real life, and if you think that's easy to come by, you must have blown a tube in your television set.

Can they all say yes to such an invitation? Of course not. When Christianity is presented whole, it not only eludes the shallow; it also frightens the timid. If it is not reduced to a pietistic ideology in support of bourgeois mediocrity, it comes through as Jesus intended it—as a call to adventure, to sacrifice, to triumph. Many of my high school students, when confronted with the stark demands of the Gospel, are wont to call such a message "idealistic" (a teen-age putdown) and to remind me that in the real world we have to be "practical" or "realistic." Such code words mask a recognition that Christianity is countercultural:

that it takes the Cross seriously and is wild enough to believe in resurrection. At which point they ring up "$ No Sale." But at least the message has been proclaimed with fidelity; and if they reject it, they are rejecting the real thing and not a childish caricature. Jesus got the same response from the rich young man when He spelled out the cost of discipleship. Evangelization does not guarantee success, only seriousness and honesty.

This brief and incomplete description of evangelization outlines a style of religious education that growing young Catholics need today, and to which many respond with heartening enthusiasm. It is clear, however, that for such a message to be convincing, it must be able to point to a quality of adult faith that youth can recognize and respect. Cultural Christianity no longer attracts; more often it bores, and sometimes positively repels. And it mocks the efforts of even the most eloquent ministers of the Word who speak to youth. A child-centered church is bound to fail, because youth's religious response is tied to the quality of adult religious experience and practice. The future does indeed belong to the young, but in the present they depend on us not only for words but even more for deeds of faith. The crisis of faith among the young is but a reflection of a deeper malaise among the old, many of whom have never been effectively evangelized themselves. It looks more and more, each year, as though we and our children shall enter the kingdom together, or not at all.

Topics for Discussion

1. Can you remember when religion, for you, ceased to be an exercise of custom or habit and became a matter of conviction and choice?

2. Do you think that young people today are capable of asking the questions that might expand their horizons and open them up to religious vision and experience?

3. Are we still a child-centered church?

Chapter Six

Telling the Jesus Story

RELIGIOUS EDUCATION, TO BE EFFECTIVE, MUST HELP YOUNG people come to a personal faith in Jesus Christ. It can take many forms and use many strategies, but at the heart of the process is the telling of the Jesus story. How can we help our students hear this tale not as a stale, familiar rerun but as a challenging personal message addressed to them here and now?

John Shea, in his *Stories of Faith* (Thomas More Press), distinguishes four orientations to Jesus—the way of admiration, the way of imitation, the way of explanation, and the way of retelling his story. Admiration leads to praise; imitation leads to the adoption of His perspectives, attitudes, and life style; and explanation leads to interest in His person. All of these have their place and their value, but they depend on the fourth way:

> Faith in Jesus means retelling the Jesus stories so that the life of the teller is interwoven with the tale. The core of the process is the interaction of two stories—the life story of the individual and the inherited story of Jesus. How can we weave together the stories of Jesus and of our students,

so that He may come across not as a remote figure from the past but as a living, present force in their lives?

The best way to start is not with the Gospel but with the young person. What is an adolescent? A person who emerges from childhood with a suitcase filled with all sorts of things: values, prejudices, hopes, fears, loyalties, aspirations. Some of this baggage will be kept, some will be discarded, as the adolescent deals with the basic questions: Who am I? What kind of person am I becoming? What kind of person do I want to be? What sort of world do I want to live in?

To the teenager or young adult confronting these questions, what does religion offer? Unfortunately, it often looks to him like a prepackaged identity, a straitjacket designed to inhibit freedom and discourage choice. How far this is from the truth can be seen if we observe Jesus in the Gospel narrative. He is constantly encountering people—rich and poor, sick and well, old and young, conventional and outcast, saint and sinner, friend and enemy. What happens when He meets them?

Well, let's first see what does not happen. They do not come away saying, "I understand my religion much better now." The Samaritan woman doesn't tell the townspeople: "I have the speaker for our next religious education workshop." Zacchaeus doesn't ask for a bibliography on business ethics. The rich young man doesn't organize a seminar on career changes. In other words, Jesus doesn't take people on head trips. He is not a philosopher, speculating on the meaning of life and submitting provisional syntheses to the criticism of his academic peers. He does not sound like a Talmudic scholar, the Jewish equivalent of a research theologian. He doesn't even sound like a conventional religious educator, dispensing religious information and testing and marking for retention. There were no half-sheet quizzes administered on the hillsides of Galilee.

Jesus doesn't come across as a cult leader, either. He asks for total commitment, but He has a scrupulous regard for freedom and self-determination. There are no seductive offers of instant friendship; no sweeping, simple solutions to life's problems and mysteries. Disciples are under no pressure to stay, and may leave at any time.

Moreover, He is not a sensitivity group facilitator. If people want to get in touch with their feelings, that's fine, but He's after bigger game. Neither has He come to affirm people uncritically: His message is much more than "I'm OK, you're OK."

Finally, and most emphatically, He is not into values clarification. He doesn't tell His hearers that their main job is to find out what's important *for them,* or that their value judgments and choices are self-justifying so long as they feel good about them.

No, Jesus is neither philosopher nor theologian nor pedagogue nor guru nor facilitator. He is not occupied in poll-taking or surveys or behavioral research. He is neither neutral nor nondirective. In short, He is none of the things that most of us religious educators have, at one time or another, tried to be.

Well, then, what *is* He?

He is a man who calls people to decision. He reveals people to themselves, helps them to see who they are and where they're going. He cuts through rationalization and self-deception. He breaks down the defenses that people throw up against self-discovery and the demands of reality. In none of this does He do violence to the freedom or the dignity of the human person. But He is unwavering in His determination to tell it like it is, no matter what the cost. If this uncompromising honesty leaves Him with few or even no disciples, then so be it. He is organizing a trip through a narrow gate, and crowds need not apply. If the rich young man cannot stand the idea of not being rich, let him stay home and count his money. If the young fishermen aren't ready to leave their nets, they're not ready to follow Him. If Peter doesn't want to hear about the Cross, he can stay in Caesarea Philippi where it's safe, but the first team is going to Jerusalem.

Love Makes Demands

In other words, discipleship costs. Sure, love sounds great, and who's against love? But this love makes demands. Sure, there's joy and victory at the end of the trail; but the way there leads through service and self-sacrifice and self-denial. There's no Easter without a Good Friday.

Can you and I, Catholic educators, honestly say that when we present the Christian message to our growing children, it sounds like this? People who opened themselves up to Jesus felt they were being summoned to a dangerous adventure with exciting possibilities. When was the last time the message of Christ sounded like that to you? When was the last time you make it sound like that? Does it sound anything like that to your kids?

Young people want to find out not only who they are, but who they could be. They hunger for ideals, even while they're afraid of them. What do we have to offer them? What does Jesus have to offer?

Zacchaeus doesn't feel good. Being a crook has made him unpopular not only with the neighbors but with himself. When he meets Jesus, he is not told: "Well, somebody has to collect the taxes. Hey, it's a dog-eat-dog world, and you gotta look out for yourself and your family. How about making a contribution to the synagogue?" No, his whole scale of values must be subverted. A whole new way of life opens up. It's not going to be easy, but with Jesus' help, he can do it. Most kids, like most grownups, would like to be honest, but not too honest . . . not if it's going to cost them money. Jesus tells me I can be honest, period. Zacchaeus proves it.

John and Andrew follow Him timidly, at a distance. Jesus asks, "What are you looking for?"

—What are we looking for? We don't even know. If we keep working for Zebedee as fishermen, we can be prosperous and comfortable, get married and have 6.4 children, expand the fishing fleet, go to synagogue every Saturday, and die of old age."

—"Well, is that what you really want?"

—"No. We thought there must be something more."

—"There is. Leave your nets and Zebedee and burn your bridges behind you, and come follow Me."

The Samaritan woman has been living a lie. Men use her; other women look down on her. She wants to discuss theology: where is the true Temple? Jesus says, "Forget the theology. Let's talk about you. When are you going to clean up your act?" He doesn't play values clarification games with her. He doesn't say her lifestyle is okay as long as she feels good about herself. Or as long as she has a meaningful relationship with the latest guy. Or so long as she's "following her conscience." He offers her affirmation, but only if she's willing to turn herself around and live the truth. So she tells her neighbors, "Come and meet a man who told me everything I ever did." How many kids to you know who need just that—to be told the truth, not to put them down, but to help them raise themselves up?

Unhappy Endings

These stories don't all turn out happily. No teacher who ever gave a good course or taught a good class and ran into a stone wall of rejection, will be surprised. Judas gets about as close to Christ as anyone could . . . and he walks away and sells Him out. The Scribes and Pharisees have Him and His marvels right in front of them, and they see nothing, because they don't want to. Pilate is fascinated by Him; but when the governor realizes that this unshakeable young Jew could interfere with his career, he washes his hands of Him. These stories with unhappy endings underline a significant fact about Jesus: When good people meet Him with open minds and hearts, they become better; but bad people with closed hearts become worse. Some of my students see this readily, but many are reluctant to admit that Jesus, or religion, could actually be bad for you. It seems almost unAmerican.

When one goes beyond pious froth and pursues considerations like these with the young, some interesting things happen. Take the case of Pilate. When we discuss his responsibility in the case of the priests vs. Jesus, the students reach remarkably diverse conclusions. Some go right to the heart of the matter, and convict him of judicial murder; once he found the defendant innocent, he should have released him without further ado. But their classmates have all kinds of problems with so straightforward a verdict. "You have to understand Pilate's problem: he was under a lot of pressure." "Jesus should have given Pilate more help; by His attitude he was really asking for trouble." "If Pilate had let Jesus go, he would have had a riot on his hands. His first job was to keep the peace." "You couldn't blame Pilate for worrying about his job, especially if he had a family to support." As Kurt Vonnegut would say, And so it goes.

If anyone ever doubted that the New Testament is relevant and very much alive, such conversations would disabuse him. The Gospel story is about *today*; the Jesus story is about *us*. The same battles between good and evil, integrity and dishonesty, justice and injustice that raged around Jesus are going on today. Then and now, people are being called upon to stand up and be counted. Are you with Jesus or against Him? Are you for human rights, or corporate profits? Do you want justice for everyone, or just for your own kind? Do you want justice even if it costs you money? They say that every man has his price. Do you? Did Jesus?

Jesus Is Bad for You?

Are these the things we talk about when we talk religion or try to teach or preach it? And if they're not . . . could this give us a hint as to why we bore people?

Can you stand one more footnote on the Pilate story? This past year, in more than one class, we were discussing which people, besides Pilate, might have been worse off for having met Jesus. They mentioned some obvious ones, like Judas and the

Pharisees. Do you know whom else they came up with? Zacchaeus. The Samaritan woman. The Apostles. That wasn't the answer I was looking for, so I asked them why. "Well, Zacchaeus had a good job and a lot of money until he met Jesus; after that, he was probably poor." "The Samaritan woman probably lost a lot of friends when she reformed." "The Apostles gave up a good business and a prosperous life, became wandering preachers and got persecuted." Two of the kids who felt sorry for Zacchaeus added saving footnotes. Said one: "He was financially worse off, but better off spiritually." Whatever *that* means! Another wrote: "But I guess he was ultimately better off, because he got to heaven." Do you get it? Following Christ is bad for you when you're alive, but it pays off after you're dead! But Jesus congratulates Zacchaeus for being an honest man and says, "*This day* salvation is come to this house." Not in heaven. Not after you're dead. This day. Now.

Sure, the Samaritan woman may have known loneliness and rejection when she changed her ways. You don't tear or rebuild a life in one day. But the day she responded to Christ she began to *live.* Now she could be the person *she* wanted to be, not the nonperson others wanted her to be. Is that so different from what our young people want and fear and need help to become?

Yes, Pilate kept his job and his villa on the Black Sea and the free chariot service. And he went down in history as a coward and a hypocrite. Are the choices that face us and our children so different?

Yes, the Apostles suffered a notable diminution in their lifestyle when they signed on with Jesus. But they sure had lots of excitement! And they were never bored again. And what half-educated fishermen and tradesmen ever did more with their lives or had a greater impact on history? Our young people are so fearful of risk, so bent on comfort and security. But there's another side to them—the side that wants to feel that their lives are significant, that they make a difference. It is this side that Jesus appealed to and brought out in the idealistic young people He met and called. He still does. Do you?

Telling the Jesus story this way does not guarantee that our students will come to faith. That is a matter of free choice. But they have a right to hear something more than vapid pieties and pious generalities. Whether they can measure up to the stark message of Jesus Christ is between them and Him.

We have been exhorted in recent years to "teach as Jesus did." This is no small task. It means offering more than vague humanism, more than religious language. It means offering a Jesus who calls to decision and commitment, who summons us to be our best selves. It means telling a story that starts anew with every human being who hears it and who has to write his or her own ending. That was Jesus' way, and no one has ever improved upon it.

Topics for Discussion

1. Is this way of thinking about Jesus familiar to you?

2. Do your young people think of Jesus as being anything like this? How *do* they imagine him?

3. Would the image of Jesus, as a man calling to decision, appeal to the young? Does it appeal to you?

Chapter 7

How They Grow and Learn

WHEN AMERICANS IN LARGE NUMBERS WORRY AND WONDER why Johnny can't read or write or spell or multiply, they create a backlash against educational innovation. Their war cry is, "Back to the basics!"

When Catholics in sufficiently large numbers worry and wonder why Johnny doesn't know the Ten Commandments, can't say his prayers and knows nothing about Mass except that he doesn't want to go, they create a backlash against catechetical innovation. Their war cry is the same: "Back to the basics!"

Because many of these dissatisfied adults have nothing more sophisticated to suggest than a return to McGuffey's Reader or the Baltimore Catechism, they are easy to ignore. Teachers of the four R's—reading, writing, 'rithmetic and religion—tend to dismiss such complaints as the wing-flapping of troglodytes. This is unfortunate. For, although some of the most vocal backlashers are reactionary, rigid and rude, they are on to something. There is a problem. Disturbingly large numbers of children and young people are growing up not only functionally illiterate, but religiously illiterate, as well.

Responsibly progressive educators are rightly concerned lest a swing of the pendulum back to the past may negate genuine progress and bring back some of the most undesirable features of the (not so) good old days. Perceptive catechists, keenly aware of the very real gains made in the religious socialization of the young since Vatican II, know that a return to some new version of the Baltimore Catechism is an ill-advised, outdated, and ultimately impossible nostalgia trip. But they should not close their eyes to facts that may no longer be denied. Too many young people graduate from school lacking the reading and writing and computational skills needed to function capably in our society. And too many youngsters emerge from Catholic schools and parish programs knowing only that "Jesus makes you feel good." Religious educators should be able to do better than that. They *must* do better, or the better part of a generation may be lost to the church, with disturbing implications for the generations that follow.

So much for the bad news. Now the good news: We *can* do better.

When things are going badly and one wants to set them right, it usually helps to start by determining where they went wrong. An adequate appraisal of the genesis and anatomy of break-up and confusion in catechetics and the larger process of religious socialization in the postconciliar church must consider two factors in that process: 1) the dissolution of the Catholic ghetto; 2) the evolving self-image of the church.

Ever since Vatican II, the American Catholic ghetto has been gradually disappearing. A few snipers still hold out in the hills, but, for the vast majority, the experience of being American and Catholic in the past 25 years has been one of cultural and religious pluralism. Even before indoctrination became undesirable, it became impossible. Conformity to social pressures can no longer ensure a stable religious identity. In a pluralistic milieu, religious identification must result from personal conviction and free choice. Needless to say, we are speaking here of adults. Children and adolescents have few convictions and make even fewer genuinely free choices. But children, even when they are under the influence of adults, must be prepared for the real world of their coming adulthood; and this means they must be prepared for a world in which their religious allegiances must be autonomous if they are to endure.

Then and Now

At the same time that the religious ghetto was breaking up, the self-image of the church was changing. Benedict Ashley once observed that the Baltimore Catechism was the right book in the right place at a certain period of the church's evolution. For the way we saw ourselves then, it was well fitted for the process of religious socialization. Today, however, our self-understanding is significantly different, not only in popular attitudes but even in conciliar documents. The vision of church in the documents of Vatican II was surely not the same as in those of Vatican I. There is continuity in the two visions, of course; but there is also a clear and dramatic evolution. We do not have a contemporary catechetical instrument to match our understanding, to do for the church of the twenty-first century what the Baltimore Catechism did for the first half of the twentieth. The new Universal Catechism which appeared in late 1992 is supposed to fulfill the need, but the prognosis is not optimistic. It looks too much like old skins for new wine.

Even if we agree on what the Gospel message is, can we communicate it faithfully and effectively to a new generation? This depends on an anterior issue that must be faced by those who instruct the young, namely: Do you *want* to teach Christian doctrine to children?

This question is not as captious as it may seem. When catechists of children and young adolescents have an adult grasp of their own faith, they experience real difficulties in expressing that faith in language suited to their charges. It is an undeniable fact that great religions speak to the deepest and most fundamental questions and longings of the human heart. The questions and longings, and even the answers, can sometimes be shared with children; but there is a genuine problem of communication arising from the significant differences in the way children and adults think and question and learn (more of this later). For the moment, let us acknowledge that, when you share adult concerns with children, their grasp of what you say may be not only limited but also distorted. This helps to explain why catechists of adolescents spend a frustratingly large part of their time doing "repair work," trying to clear up misunderstandings and caricatures.

This almost—but not quite—justifies the ensuing reluctance of some religious educators to persist in a losing cause. It accounts for the tendency of many postconciliar religion programs to be very thin on content. One result of this approach is galloping religious illiteracy among adolescents. It goes far beyond not being able to rattle off the Ten Commandments, the Twelve Apostles, the Gifts of the Holy Spirit and the Seven Deadly Sins. Too many young Catholics, after eight or 12 years in Catholic schools or parish instructional programs, come up short not only on fundamental religious information but also on basic skills, like praying and celebrating. They are unable to participate in the life of the church, and lack the skills needed to catch up. They cannot feel themselves part of the story of our tribe when they have not even heard that story.

Children must be put in touch with the religious tradition of their community. That is how socialization works, whether religious or secular. When we socialize American children, we tell them about the colonists and about Washington and Jefferson and Lincoln. We teach them to salute the flag and to sing the national anthem. We insist that they have a rudimentary knowledge of the Declaration of Independence and the U. S. Constitution. That's not jingoism; that's getting back to the basics of citizenship. There will be a time for more critical understanding and a sense of history later on, in high school and college and beyond.

The same applies to the task of socializing a Catholic child. A way must be found to put youngsters in living touch with the religious tradition of their family and community. Obviously, this should include affective, as well as cognitive, learning, experiences of prayer and celebration and the imparting of skills and competencies needed to participate in the life of the church. These can be developed and refined later on. But there must be some knowledge to develop and some skills to refine, or youth ministers will be working in a vacuum.

But the question remains: Can we share an adult religion with children? The problem is particularly acute for Catholics who, in the last twenty-five years, have consciously strived for, and often achieved, a more mature level of religious faith and practice. It is not an exaggeration to say that, in the aftermath of Vatican II, many Roman Catholics grew up. For proof, we need look no further than to the all-too-evident growing pains. One troubling consequence has been their inability to communicate effectively with their children on a religious level. The old catechism formulas satisfy neither them nor their children. What can be put in their place?

There is more than one answer to this question. What is needed is not a cure-all but an unlocking key, a standard by which we can evaluate and refine existing and future programs of religious instruction and formation.

When most church people seek such a key, they look to the bishops or theologians. In doing so, they are concentrating on the content of the message. Is this presentation of doctrine faithful to God's self-revelation? Is it orthodox? Does it make use of the best theological insights and research? This is proper, but they must go further and ask other questions. How do children grow and learn? How does the immaturity of the child or the maturity of the adult affect the perception and appropriation of religious truth? It is time to do scientifically what we have always tried to do by instinct or hunch: to adapt our teaching and preaching to the capacity of the child or youth.

The Developmentalist Approach

We are now in a position to do this, thanks to the work of developmentalists like the late Lawrence Kohlberg and James Fowler. Building on the work of such men as John Dewey, Jean Piaget and Erik Erikson, they have made valuable contributions to educational theory which have important implications for the church's teaching ministry.

Although Kohlberg's work has come in for a great deal of criticism, much of it deserved, moral educators in large numbers attest to the value of his theory in constructing, administering and evaluating methods and programs of moral formation.

Basic to his system is the developmentalists' premise that human beings proceed through certain predictable stages of growth on the way to, and through, maturity, and that these stages cannot be skipped. Thus, for example, children must pass through an initial preconventional, or premoral, phase, wherein right and wrong are seen as the arbitrary construction of big people, or perceived crudely in terms of reward and punishment. Only later can they understand or assimilate exhortations to moral behavior based on social considerations, like the needs or expectations of the group or community (conventional morality). And this level of moral judgment may be (but is not always) eventually superseded by a higher, postconventional level, where ethical judgments and decisions are made on the basis of universal principles.

This writer is one of many thousands of educators personally indebted to him for providing a basis and structure for clarifying goals and pursuing realistic objectives in programs of moral education. Moreover, it works not only with children, but also with adults. Anyone working in the Christian ministry needs all the help he or she can get in gauging and interpreting the receptivity of adult congregations to moral preaching and motivation. And the assistance provided by Kohlberg is of very high value. He helps us to adapt our presentation to the capacity of our listeners, whether children or grown-ups, and also provides strategic guidelines for helping them move up the ladder of moral maturity.

One small example may be in order. For many years in working with teenagers, I have been encouraging them to be honest and to respect the rights and property of others. Time and again, in discussing cases of injustice to others, I found it disconcerting and frustrating to hear students say, "I'd give the money back if I knew the owner," or "I'd try to do something [about an injustice] if it was being done to friends of mine." Kohlberg helped me to see that such limitations were often due not to insensitivity, but to immaturity; that appeals to principled thinking are often lost on the young, precisely because they are young. Such examples could be multiplied over and over.

Fowler, a disciple of Kohlberg, converted a brilliant hunch into a theory of faith development that can enlighten and enrich not only religious education but the whole spectrum of Christian ministry. He, too, works within the developmental system, and attempts to show, through careful research and interpretation, that people go through predictable stages of faith even as they proceed through stages of moral development. The accent is on growth and maturity. If Fowler is right, his theory is of universal validity and not limited to particular cultures. And it applies not only to Christian, or even theistic, faith, but to any belief (or unbelief) system. He uses a broad definition of faith, as a mode of being in relation to what is conceived of as one's ultimate environment. Whether one is a Christian, a Buddhist, a humanist or even an agnostic, that person will pass through predictable phases and transitions and will exhibit certain characteristics and behavior proper to each stage of development. A brief synopsis of some of these stages may give an incomplete but helpful overview of the stage theory.

Stages of Faith

Somewhere between the ages of six and 11, the child leaves what Fowler calls the "intuitive-projective" stage and arrives at the second or "mythic-literal" stage. Thought is gradually freed from the domination of perception and feeling, but is still tied to the concrete world of sensory experience. This is the story-telling stage, in which myths rather than abstract concepts are employed to express the ultimate environment. The acceptance of such myths is, by and large, uncritical. Abstract doctrinal formulations can be memorized and "given back," but the intellectual grasp of these formulas is severely limited. If you don't believe it, ask any priest who ever tried to preach at a children's Mass and didn't have any stories to tell.

The transition to the third or "synthetic-conventional" stage, occurs toward the end of childhood. This stage, which may last only until the late teens or may persist right through middle age, is a "conformist" phase, characterized by keen awareness of the expectations and judgments of others. A person in stage three is not sufficiently autonomous to take an independent stance toward his or her own beliefs and values. The latter may be deeply felt, and the person may live and act quite consistently with them. But they are grounded on the authority of a person or of a group consensus, and that authority is perceived as self-evidently valid, not subject to appeal.

Even the casual reader will recognize in Fowler's synthetic-conventional stage many features of: Kohlberg's conventionally moral person, the uncritical patriot, the unquestioning loyalist, the "true believer." It is also a strikingly accurate description of the kind of Catholic who dominated the pre-Vatican II church.

For a description of the "new" Catholics who emerged in such unprecedented numbers in the wake of the council, we need only turn to Fowler's fourth stage, the "independent-reflexive." The transition to this stage may begin as early as the late teens, or much later, or perhaps not at all. Stage four is characterized by a newly autonomous perspective, as the individual becomes less dependent on others to construct and maintain his world of meaning. He feels newly aware of his personal responsibility for that faith, and places a high value on authenticity and consistency. Fowler insists that such autonomy is not necessarily individualistic. Still, it is clear that those in stage four, whether they work for companies, serve in armies or belong to churches, are going to be a threat to those in stage three, especially when the latter remain fixated at that stage of development long past young adulthood. Such an analysis goes far to explain the painful dislocations and polarizations that have afflicted the church in the years since the Council.

The Vatican I church, with its strong discipline and its stress on obedience to authority and institutional loyalty, inhibited and even stifled the normal transition from stage three to four. For better or for worse, the church now has a large population of independent-reflexive members, many of whom are priests and a few of whom even occasionally become bishops. The religious educator must make a value judgment on such developments. If he or she feels about stage four the way the apostle Peter felt about the Mount of Transfiguration—"Lord, it is good for us to be here"—she will make plans in her goals and curriculum and teaching style for a timely and orderly transition to what she sees as a mature, responsible kind of adult faith. If, on the other hand, she feels, rather, that this last state is worse than the first, she will try to head off at the pass any movement toward autonomy and independence, and will stress obedience and loyalty as the desirable end products of orthodox religious formation.

This is not the place to describe at any length the later steps on Fowler's ladder of faith maturity, which occur only well into adult years. In brief, the fifth or "paradoxical-consolidative" stage, rarely (if ever) occurs before the age of 30. This is the person who esteems the independence and authenticity of stage four, but who now tries to keep these values in fruitful tension with the more stable qualities of stage three, such as obedience, loyalty and dependence. Stage-five individuals think more dialectically, resonate positively to tension and paradox and are at home with ambiguity and mystery. People at this stage often become peacemakers between members of stages three and four, and the Catholic Church never needed them more than it does now.

This sketchy and, I must insist, incomplete, excursion through the world of ideas and values inhabited by Kohlberg and Fowler and their disciples, may stimulate parents, pastors, teachers and youth ministers to clarify the goals, objectives and strategies they employ in the religious nurture of the young. Religious educators, in particular, are offered an unparalleled opportunity to bring order and academic respectability into a field that has lately been long on enthusiasm and insight, but short on structure and clarity of long-range purpose.

Limits of Theory

Kohlberg does not tell us what is right or wrong, nor does he indulge in value judgments on what is virtuous and what is sinful. As a psychologist, he cannot play that role. But he does tell us much about how children and youths and adults think and feel and judge and decide in matters moral; and he provides for moral educators a set of sequential objectives, an instrument for evaluation and the raw material for the elaboration of effective strategies and methods.

Similarly, when Fowler works within the limits of his discipline, he does not tell us which faith is true, nor does he pass value judgments on the validity of various formulations of Christian doctrine. He himself is a committed and devout Christian, whose personal life is marked by a strong current of prayer and solid piety. But his theory, as such, is broadly ecumenical in the sense that it helps people of all persuasions to understand themselves and their individual journeys of faith. And religious educators who appreciate and utilize his insights can avoid many mistakes and dead ends in communicating with the young.

Today, all over the country, parish coordinators, high-school religion department chairpersons and diocesan directors of religious education are being challenged by pastors, principals, parents and prelates. The questioners are sometimes strident, more often restrained; but they are becoming more and more urgent. They want to know: What are you trying to do? What are the bases of your programs? What are your long-range goals? What is the rationale for your curriculum sequence, your strategies, your methods? When the controversy centers on content, authoritative teaching and theological resources must be consulted. But, in other aspects of this issue, developmental psychology offers a rich mine of constructive assistance. Wherever religious educators may locate themselves on the spectrum of Catholic attitudes—whether radical or liberal or progressive or conservative—they cannot ignore solid scholarship and enlightenment about how children grow and learn.

Developmental psychology, by itself, does not provide answers to all the problems confronting religious education. But the maturation of work done by men like. Kohlberg and Fowler comes at just the time when the most creative catechists can make the best use of it. Good things are happening in many school and parish religious programs; among the more successful of these, what is often lacking is only a sense of structure, of overall unity of thrust, of a pedagogic theory that could give coherence to the whole enterprise. Kohlberg and Fowler do not lay it all out in finished form, but they provide the tools for its construction. It only remains for the leaders in Catholic religious education to meet the challenge and seize the opportunity.

"Back to the basics" does not have to be a shibboleth of reactionary obscurantism. It could be the rallying cry of the best and the brightest as they try to heed the Lord's injunction to let the little ones come to Him, for of such is the kingdom of heaven.

Topics for Discussion

1. Would you agree that, in the years following Vatican II, adult American Catholics grew up?

2. Do you see any of your own story in the developmentalists' descriptions of stages of faith and moral maturity?

3. Do the descriptions of these stages throw light on any of your experiences in trying to teach the young?

Chapter 8

Teaching Right and Wrong (I)

RIDDLE: WHICH THREE LITTLE WORDS WERE HARDLY EVER HEARD in Catholic religion classes thirty years ago, are heard more and more every year, mean different things to adults and youngsters, can express theological depth or religious shallowness, bring joy to adolescents, heartburn to parents, distress to pastors and sadness to popes?

If you answered "Follow your conscience," go to the head of the class.

'Twas not always thus. In the good old days, religion teachers told kids what they should and should not do. That's what teachers were for, to tell students things they needed to know. Parents sent their children to Catholic school or to confraternity classes in the expectation that there they would learn "the difference between right and wrong." Some parents still do. And so do some teachers. And some children. But some strange things are going on today, disguised as moral education but sometimes causing serious confusion.

Indoctrination and Values-Clarification

It all started when indoctrination, or "brainwashing," became undesirable in Catholic and other educational circles. The rejection of authoritarianism was and is a healthy phenomenon, to be applauded and encouraged. If there was any doubt on this score, one had only to think through the implications of the Nuremberg trials and the My Lai massacre to see that the responsible exercise of conscience is preferable to mindless obedience. "Good Germans" need no longer apply. The Second Vatican Council and its aftermath encouraged this development, albeit somewhat ambiguously (as it did almost everything). The storm that followed *Humanae Vitae* underlined the need for educating people to make decisions of personal conscience. And when Gordon Liddy led the "good soldiers" of the Watergate conspiracy into jail, we felt vindicated once again.

Enter Sidney Simon and the values-clarification people. They had some good things to say about helping young people to clarify the values that move them and shape their behavior. They offered many helpful strategies which teachers could use successfully. Their stuff *worked*, with remarkable frequency. Students were no longer parroting back the moral preachments of teachers, but were digging within themselves and coming up with value judgments that carried personal conviction. But there were problems. Sometimes youngsters arrived at ideas and decisions which to adults seemed irresponsible and dangerous. The latter wanted to challenge and sometimes even contradict those judgments, but they hesitated. The values-clarification theoreticians gave them no encouragement, and understandably so. For the whole thrust of their philosophy and method is not to help the student find the *truth*, but to find *his* or *her* truth. It is not objectivity that is being sought, but sincerity. So what do you tell the student who decides in favor of abortion? Or premarital sex? Or cheating or stealing? If you insist on imposing your own values, will you not thereby stifle the process of growth toward individual responsibility? On the other hand, do you not have a duty to offer clear moral guidance to those younger and less experienced than yourself? Doesn't moral leadership demand un-equivocal witness to the truth?

The Problem

Before we offer our resolution of this dilemma, let us state the main thesis of this chapter. There are large numbers of religious educators in our schools and parish programs who have either not faced this problem squarely or who have come up with answers that are not only irreconcilable with authentic Catholic teaching but are bad education and dangerous to their students.

We are not talking about the authoritarians, the heavy-handed pedagogues who stifle initiative and "lay down the law." These are usually well-intentioned people who are keenly aware of youth's limitations and who wish to protect them from doing harm to themselves or others. They honestly believe that the way to prevent children from getting bad ideas is to give them good ones and to discourage argument. They get away with it for a while, until the kids reach the ripe old age of 12 or 13, and the backlash sets in. Then, until high school graduation, it's either "War" or the game known as "Play It Cool and Don't Let Them See Your Cards." And, after graduation, the lid is off forever and ever, Amen.

No, we're not talking about the authoritarians. We will always have them with us, and they will always create their own kinds of problems. Our concern is with the folks at the other end of the spectrum. These try so hard to avoid the pitfalls just described that they dig another set of holes just as deep and just as perilous. They start with some very good insights and values. They believe in the dignity of conscience, the worth of the individual, the need for people to do their own thinking. They eschew irresponsibility disguised as loyalty. Their enemies list is peopled by drill sergeants, generals, puritans, bigots, chauvinists and hardhat patriots. They dream of a world inhabited by individuals of conscience and conviction, and see education as a liberating process leading to such a world. They are optimistic, they believe in people and they want people to feel good about themselves, starting when they're young.

"Don't Show Your Cards"

So, where do they go wrong?

Some fail their children because they fear confrontation with them. They are so afraid of appearing uptight that they tiptoe around areas of disagreement. They think that if they contradict the young they will lose them. Many of these timid souls are also painfully aware that in the recent past they warned their children against some things which they now consider either harmless or even desirable, and they don't want to send people on any more gratuitous guilt trips.

Others err in more subtle ways. They want young people to develop personal convictions and to opt for a life style based not on fear or conformity but on genuinely free choice. They perceive, correctly, that in a world of cultural pluralism people can depend less and less on social pressure and approval and must develop a set of values that are truly their own. In a word, they want their children to grow up *free*. And how, they ask, can you be free when adults are always telling you what to do? So they leave them alone. Oh, I don't mean that they abandon them. They still gather them together in religion classrooms, in parish programs, in retreat settings, and discuss moral issues with them. Questions are raised. Opinions are solicited. Judgments are expressed and stands are taken—but not by the teachers. Oh, no. To tell the kids what *you* think is a sure way to kill a good discussion. How can they clarify their values if you keep intruding and imposing your own? So if they ask you if you think abortion is wrong, don't tell them where you stand; find out where *they* stand, and why. If they assert that stealing is all right so long as you do it from big stores or rich people, don't reject their opinion. If they ask you your opinion on premarital sex, tell them it all depends. Don't break up the game by showing them your cards.

Being Responsible

To be sure, this kind of response has much to recommend it, at least at the outset. Youngsters should be encouraged to use their own cognitive and affective resources to search for truth and not settle too easily for pat, ready-made solutions provided by authority figures. There are a host of good reasons why teachers and other youth guides should encourage independent thinking. The really skillful teacher is the one who can structure learning situations in such a way that the truth is discovered rather than imposed. For that is how values are interiorized and become operative in the lives of people who prefer to choose their way of life rather than simply live up to other people's expectations. But what should a responsible adult do when the discussion has run its course, the group is tired of the subject and it's time to move on, but some youngsters are still on record as favoring ideas or courses of action that you consider potentially destructive?

That is the time to say something like this: "Well, we have had a very interesting discussion about stealing (or cheating, or abortion, or premarital sex, etc.), and we haven't arrived at a consensus. I'm glad that you feel free, in this class. to express your honest feelings and opinions, to disagree with one another and to disagree with me. So what I'm going to say now is not meant as a put-down. I think you're wrong. As a Christian and as a human being, I reject not you but your opinion. I believe that the conclusions you have reached are dangerous and potentially destructive. Act on them, and you may hurt yourself and others. I know you don't see it this way, and I don't question your sincerity. I don't want you to say things you don't believe, or to stop thinking for yourself. I don't even deny that possibly— just *possibly*—you may some day be proven right, and I may be proven wrong. But meanwhile, I have a responsibility to myself and to you to stand up for what I believe and to caution you against behavior that I consider irresponsible. I have to do this, because I love you, I care about you and I take you seriously."

If we do less than this . . . if we content ourselves merely with eliciting opinions from the young, and fail to challenge and even contradict them. . . we abdicate moral leadership. We expose ourselves to the same charges that William Bennett, then Secretary of Education, made against public schools' attempts at sex education. Because of the taboo on teaching any kind of morality, curriculum guides show how to help students "explore options," "evaluate the choices involved," "identify alternative actions," and "examine their own values" . . . and nothing more.

> What's wrong with this kind of teaching? First, it is a very odd kind of teaching—very odd because it does not teach. It does not teach because, while speaking to a very important aspect of human life, it displays a conscious aversion to making moral distinctions. Indeed, it insists on holding them in abeyance. The words of morality, of a rational, mature morality, seem to have been banished from this sort of sex education.
>
> To do what is being done in these classes is tantamount to throwing up our hands and saying to our young people: "We give up. We give up on teaching right and wrong to you. Here, take these facts, take this information, and take your feelings, your options, and try to make the best decisions you can. But you're on your own. We can say no more." It is ironic that, in the part of our children's lives where they may most need adult guidance, and where indeed I believe they most want it, too often the young find instead an abdication of responsible moral authority.[1]

Educators in public schools may plead, in their defense, that they are not allowed to do more. But what's our excuse?

Respecting the Laws of Growth

If you still have trouble with this kind of approach and are still not convinced of its wisdom, recall some of the basic insights of developmentalists like Kohlberg and Fowler.

Dr. Kohlberg, in describing the third rung on his ladder of moral maturity, calls it the "good boy/girl" stage. At this level, moral judgments are decisively influenced by the significant others. The latter, for younger children, will be adults, especially parents. For teen-agers, it will often be their peers. When adult authorities follow a hands-off policy and decline to take a stand on moral issues, they may think they are freeing them for autonomous decision making, but are actually only yielding the field to others less experienced and often less wise than themselves. For example, when adults tell Stage Three adolescents to "make up their own minds" about premarital sex, they are often imposing an impossible task. Acting under the illusion of freedom, they then follow the surrogate authorities—peers, television, movies, music and magazines. True, we should not leave youngsters at Stage Three; Kohlberg encourages us to promote their growth toward Stage Four and beyond to levels of postconventional maturity. But what do we do in the meantime—abdicate responsibility? In the face of a veritable epidemic of teen-age pregnancy, venereal disease and abortion, is this the best we can do?

Dr. Fowler, in his studies of faith development, may have the answer. His analysis of Stage Four, the independent-reflexive phase, is most relevant here. When people move from the uncritical conformism of the synthetic-conventional Stage Three to the more autonomous Four, they are prone to undervalue some of the very positive features of the stage left behind. Fowler's Fours, in their newfound commitment to personal authenticity, may reject the more communal virtues like loyalty, stability, obedience. Only in the later paradoxical-consolidative Stage Five will they think more dialectically, resonate positively to tension and paradox and be at home with ambiguity and mystery. Thus, until Fours arrive at this dynamic personal synthesis, they are liable to misread signals from the young. The latter, impatient at restraint, demand "freedom," which for them means a world in which "nobody tells us what to do." For the responsible adult, on the other hand, freedom means liberation from inner restraints, as well—the ability to rise above one's own egoism to meet the demands of personal integrity. The adult who misses the difference will overestimate the young person's capacity for self-direction and will be loathe to offer the guidance that is still needed.

This seems to be what is happening in many religious education settings today. Adults who have lately graduated to a more mature level of faith-living are failing to perceive the real needs of the young who, at a much less advanced stage of development, need strong, positive leadership. This is not a call for a return to indoctrination, but a plea to religious educators to respect the laws of growth and not lay upon the young burdens too heavy for them to bear. Tell them where you and the church stand. Stand up for the truth, in season and out of season. Dare to risk unpopularity, even rejection. If you really respect your students, pay them the compliment of occasionally disagreeing with them. Many of them unconsciously want, more than anything else, to have some adult say "no," to be forthright enough to set the limits they cannot yet set for themselves.

We can learn a valuable lesson from the phenomenon of young people turning to total-control groups like the Moonies and the Children of God. The typical profile that is emerging is that of youths who are given more freedom than they can handle, who become disoriented and directionless, and in desperation turn over to others the total control of their lives, including their minds.

So should we tell the young to follow their conscience? Yes, but show them how to form a conscience . . . and make sure you know how to do it yourself. Remember that "following one's conscience" means different things to different people. To Kohlberg's postconventional, it means doing the right, no matter what the cost. To the conventional, it may mean: "Don't listen to anyone: you're on your own." And to the preconventional, it may simply mean "the lid's off; do as you please." Which of these meanings come through to your students when you use those three little words?

Topics for Discussion

1. Have the authoritarians gone the way of the dinosaur, or are they still in business?

2. Do you agree with the basic thesis of this article, that the backlash against authoritarianism has gone too far? Do you have any examples or stories to back up your view?

3. What does "following your conscience" mean to you?

Notes

1. "Sex and the Education of Our Children," *America*, 14 Feb. 1987.

Chapter 9

Teaching Right and Wrong (II)

YOUNG PEOPLE IN THEIR TEEN YEARS ARE FACED WITH CERTAIN basic tasks in their growth as persons. They must find out who they are, what they believe in, and what kind of people they want to be. They must decide what kind of world they want to live in, and how they are to be a part of that world. Toward these ends, it is desirable that they consciously choose a set of values, interiorize them, and through choices and repeated acts strive to live in a manner consistent with those values. Education should help youth make these free, responsible choices of the ideas and the values by which they live.

If, as my students say, God catches so much static for letting people choose their own world, then teachers must expect no better treatment. When you free people to choose, you take the risk of having them choose badly, sometimes with devastating consequences to themselves and others. This is the danger that impels authoritarian societies and institutions to deny their subjects the freedom they might misuse. Every school has to face this dilemma: Do we loosen the reins, give students the chance to fail, and live with a certain amount of academic inefficiency, or do we protect them from their laziness, insulate them from the consequences of their lack of self-discipline, and take upon ourselves a responsibility too heavy for the shoulders of the young?

Before you conclude that young people who have cast off the shackles of intimidation by parents, school, and church are now free to choose their own values and lifestyle, consider the following sequence of events which used to take place in my classes every year. The students were eleventh and twelfth grade boys of varied racial, ethnic and economic backgrounds from various points in and around New York City. I would show them a film debating the pros and cons of premarital sex. In that film Albert Ellis makes the following statement:

> I would like them (teens) really to stop and think for them-
> selves and ask themselves why they should or should not
> have intercourse or any other type of sex relations before
> marriage—not because their parents or other authorities
> told them not to but because they can figure out for them-
> selves the advantages and the individual disadvantages in
> each of their particular cases.

When I would solicit student reactions to Ellis' view, the comments were invariably approving, even enthusiastic. So I would ask them: Who are these authorities who are trying to make you do it their way? Together we would list them on the chalk board under Column I: Parents, School, Church. Someone would usually add, "Other Kids." And with a little prodding on my part, we would come up with a whole new team under Column II: Peers, Music, TV, Radio, Magazines, Movies.

Are the people in Column II "authorities"? You bet. And do they give you the same advice, send out the same signals, and promote the same values as those in Column I? Hell, no. Well, which group do you listen to? Now you're getting close to the knuckle. Albert Ellis is a smart man, but he said a dumb thing. He helped reinforce the illusion that when people throw off a tyrant, they are free. He ought to know that most revolutions just substitute one oppressor for another. So it is with the sexual revolution. Young people have successfully freed themselves from the authority of parents, church, and school. Now they live under the not-so-benevolent tyranny of peers, disc jockeys, and unscrupulous script writers who make money by manipulating a whole generation's fear of the ultimate put-down—sexual inadequacy.

In such a situation, what is a teacher or a parent to do? Abdicate responsibility, pretend not to notice, support by silence the illusion that all is well? Or withdraw into the castle and pull up the drawbridge? Is there no other way?

There is. If the young cannot accept our convictions on our word, we can extend a hand and help them find their own. If we cannot make them believe what we believe or choose what we choose, we can help them learn to choose. With eyes wide open, without overestimating their wisdom or their strength, we can second their stumbling efforts to be free.

Surmountable Obstacles

Of course there are problems with such an approach. I have been describing a kind of dialogue with youth, a dynamic interaction wherein we take them seriously, challenge their premises, examine options, and help them to make free, responsible choices. Even before Lawrence Kohlberg shared with us the results of his research, we knew that such a process poses many difficulties. If a person operates habitually at the preconventional level of moral maturity, basing judgments and decisions purely on fear and self-interest, such a conversation is difficult to carry on and has limited prospects of success in the short run.

Real as these problems are, they should not make us despair. The logical conclusion seems to be that we must help prod young people along toward post-conventional moral levels at a somewhat faster pace than we have done up until now. That's a hard saying, but what are the alternatives? When men and women live in a pluralistic society where authoritarianism is rejected and social pressures are blunted, the individual bears a heavier burden of choice. If the person does not yield to manipulation by subtle group pressures, he or she must choose, in terms of his or her own values, among the many possibilities open. But that is a fair description of an *adult* way of doing things. Moreover, if Kohlberg is correct in his judgment that most adults do not advance beyond Stage Four moral thinking, the picture is even more bleak, but not hopeless—not if we start, boldly and with determination, to educate the young not for conformity but for responsible freedom.

How can we stimulate the process of growth toward post-conventional moral maturity? By structuring learning situations and creating a process that encourages such growth. For several years now my students and I have been engaged in this enterprise, and the interaction produced in the classroom has been occasionally disheartening, sometimes puzzling, often encouraging, and always enlightening.

Basically, my students and I study and engage in Socratic dialogue concerning several real-life people who in the present and recent past have had to struggle with conflicts between their loyalty to nation, institutions, and laws, and their personal feelings and convictions about right and wrong. Through reflection on their struggles, occasional role-playing, and group discussion, we try to assimilate in a personal way the mentality and the values of those who act for reasons of integrity, and to understand and sympathize with those who are unable to take a critical stance toward authority. The goal is to assist the students not only to understand and appreciate, but also to move toward interiorizing a moral style based on principle and personal conviction rather than blind obedience, peer pressure, or selfishness.

One of the exercises centers around the My Lai massacre. At the close of a film detailing the horrors of the Nazi concentration camps, the narrator remarks that too many people think these things happened long ago, at a certain time in a certain place and are a thing of the past. They deceive themselves, he says, for "the monster is still alive, and in our midst." This cryptic statement elicits no clear reaction until we view a disturbing documentary film, an interview with five American soldiers who were at My Lai. This has by far the greatest impact on the groups as a whole, and produces a whole spectrum of emotional reactions, debates and discussions for weeks after.

As the five veterans describe, objectively and dispassionately, what happened on that day of shame, they repeatedly bear witness to the utter needlessness of the slaughter. Time and again we are told by eyewitnesses and participants that there was no resistance, no return fire, no threat to themselves on the part of the villagers. They remark on how many of the men were actually *enjoying* themselves, taking out their anxieties and frustrations in savage reprisal against helpless civilians. Some of the students are shocked, angry, and ashamed, as any sensitive person would be. These now perceive that "the monster" was not annihilated at Nuremberg, but lives on in our own people, in young American men who, if they had never gone to war, would probably have led normal lives free of violence and savagery.

For these students, this experience appears to be either a turning point or a moment of confirmation in their progress toward post-conventional thinking. It would be unwise to set too much store by a few weeks in a classroom, but I get the definite impression that this process, touching them not only intellectually but also emotionally, can have a significant impact on impressionable young minds and hearts. It is not just the violence of the slaughter that moves them, but the chilling rationalizations of one particular G.I. who says, over and over again, that this is what a soldier is trained to do, that he need not consider the morality of orders unless he is an officer, that orders must be carried out without question. They heard these same words uttered by the defendants at Nuremberg in pitiful justification of sickening war crimes. I like to think that when my students put all those things together, they will be much less docile and manageable if they are ever called upon to commit "legal" crimes in the name of duty or loyalty.

I wish I could report that only these positive results emerge from the study of My Lai. Alas, the outcomes are much more ambiguous. There are students who bring to the experience such strong nationalistic bias that they cannot hear what the veterans are telling them with brutal frankness. They have swallowed a thousand cliches and rationalizations, and these block out enlightenment. "I heard that children used to walk up to our soldiers and blow them up with concealed weapons." "The communists did much worse things than we did." "Civilians often booby-trapped our men." "The soldiers had to do what they were told; they had no choice."

There is another reaction to the My Lai revelations which is even more disturbing. It is the inability of many students to react at all. This is one of those phenomena that Kohlberg does not help me to evaluate. It has nothing to do with rationalization. It is a failure to *feel.*

There is a curiously low-key quality about young audiences' emotional reactions to films which shock their elders. I am not speaking of the kind of shock that is produced by the merely outspoken or unconventional. Too many adults are shocked by too many harmless things, and the youngsters don't need that kind of sensitivity. No, I mean the healthy kind of shock and dismay that normal persons experience when they witness violence and brutality.

Overloaded Circuits?

With each passing year, I find myself, after viewing a powerful documentary film with my classes, first asking the boys not what they think about the film but what they feel. I very rarely get an answer expressing emotion. Usually they proceed to tell me what they think.

Well, adults do this, too, but in a different way. My contemporaries tend to intellectualize because most of them have not been taught or encouraged to get in touch with their feelings. But the *feelings* are there, waiting to be dredged up, brought out into the open, and dealt with. With the young, it's a different story. I get the eerie but definite impression that they can't express their feelings because they don't have any. Maybe their circuits are overloaded. Maybe they've been exposed to too much too soon, through visual media. Does this sound paranoid? Then spend an hour with a group of teenagers, trying to elicit and deal with basic human emotions like pity, indignation, enthusiasm, fear, and admiration. It can be very difficult, and after a while you get the feeling that the problem is not with the medium but with the subjects. They are curiously passive and apathetic, like prematurely burnt-out cases. Whatever the explanation, the implications for moral education are not encouraging. We cannot cultivate moral perception without a foundation of basic sensitivity.

Since I teach in a Roman Catholic school, I cannot leave the issue of conscience and authority without dealing with the role of individual conviction within the Church. This is a delicate question that is hard even for adults to handle; all the more difficult is it for young people who are not always capable of nuanced thought and the fine distinctions necessary for anyone who seriously wishes to do justice to the legitimate demands both of Church authority and of individual conscience. Prudence and skill, clarity of thought, and genuine humility are required of the adult Catholic who would explain to the young how they are called to grow up responsible adults in a religious community which claims divine sanction for its exercise of leadership.

The adolescent mind, left to itself, tends to think in black-and-white, either-or categories, e.g., Are you going to follow the Church or your conscience? Some too easily accept the popular misconception of Catholic moral life as a no-win proposition in which only two choices are available: either abdicate responsibility in the name of obedience, or reject all authority in the name of freedom. This inadequate view is not limited to teenagers. Many adult Catholics have not achieved a dynamic synthesis of the roles of conscience and authority in their personal lives; some of these even make their living as priests and bishops. But we refuse to be discouraged. There is hope for the future, and its name is youth. It is well worth the risk and the trouble to explain to young adults that as grown-up Catholics they will be responsible for their own existence, that no authority can lift from their shoulders the burden of choice. Being a Catholic is a great blessing, for those who exercise the teaching office are obliged to guide and challenge us in the name of Christ. For our part, we are obliged in his name to heed their voice, to stand humbly before God, to listen to his Spirit in Scripture, in prayer, and in dialogue with the Christian community. But then we must decide, for we are free with the freedom of the sons and daughters of God. To put it in Kohlbergese: Yes, Virginia, there is a place for post-conventional people in the Catholic Church.

Most of the exercises we do in class confront problems of universal concern, in terms neither specifically Christian nor even explicitly religious. Questions like premarital sex, civil disobedience, abortion, honesty, and amnesty are not the private preserve of any religious group. Moreover, it is inadequate to try to solve any of these problems by appealing to Church dogma. The reflective, responsible adult cannot reject abortion just because "the Catholic Church is against it." If premarital sex is wrong, it cannot be wrong simply because "we have a commandment against it." The Second Vatican Council can't make saturation bombing wrong by condemning it. Lying, cheating, and stealing aren't immoral because "they're against my religion."

One inescapable conclusion is that humanity is not a given, but an achievement. Personhood is a task, and morality is an accomplishment. This is not as self-evident as it may seem at first sight. Some people think that we are naturally good, and that rascals are people who went wrong. It seems more accurate to say that wicked people are those who have failed the task of growth. Criminals are not deviants, but dropouts from the school of life.

The educator is summoned to create and shape an environment calculated to assist moral development. This is done by structuring learning situations that will promote the growth of authentic, fully functioning, responsible human beings. Parents don't send their children to school just to have their behavior analyzed; they want them to be influenced and changed for the better. Schools probably cannot succeed in opposition to familial influences which are nearly always stronger. But they can support and supplement and even make up for some of the deficiencies in home training.

In authoritarian societies those charged with the socialization of youth may attempt to accomplish this through indoctrination. Values and standards of behavior are imposed and backed up by social pressure and threats of punishment. Such tactics may succeed for a time with subjects who operate at a pre-conventional or conventional level of moral maturity, but only in a ghetto or similar closed society. A minority of today's youth, seeking a painless route to instant identity, seek to create such societies in rigid, fundamentalistic communities which specialize in thought control and offer total security to anyone willing to become a zombie. They haunt street corners and bus terminals and airports, harassing bystanders and offering "free" religious trash in exchange for a "contribution." They are pathetic and deserve our concern, but they are outside the mainstream of American life. Most of our growing children are marching to far different drummers.

To these young people, growing up in a confusing culture that features a babble of voices and unprecedented powers of manipulation, education should offer the chance to grow up responsible, sensitive, and free. Those who would engage in such a task need large stores of wisdom, inventiveness, courage, and conviction.

Topics for Discussion

1. Can young people allow themselves to feel moral indignation when it is so important to them to be "cool"?

2. Is unquestioning obedience ever desirable?

3. How do you, in your life as an adult Catholic, reconcile the demands of conscience and of church authority?

Chapter 10

Public Schools and Moral Development

Most of this book about religious and moral education presupposes church-sponsored environments such as Catholic schools, CCD programs, and parish youth groups. What about public schools? Can they play a role in this enterprise? Obviously, religious education is out of the question, except for occasional courses *about* religion. (Actually, they could do more than this without violating the reasonable separation of church and state, but that is another story, and this is not the place to go into it). What about moral education? Do those of us whose children attend public schools, have a right to expect any help from those institutions?

Most parents and other adults have paradoxical expectations of public schools. They hope that, besides teaching children to read and write and develop the other skills that will enable them to do the world's work, these institutions will also impart ideals, promote integrity, and contribute positively to character development. On the other hand, they object to any proselytizing or indoctrination. Schools are supposed to assist moral development but not "impose" values on children and young people.

They do not think that these expectations are contradictory, because they assume a societal consensus about a set of standards that are nonreligious and agreed upon by all decent people: for example, lying, stealing, violence, and abuse are bad: honesty, fairness, self-discipline, and industriousness are good. To some extent they are correct. The consensus does exist, and many children are helped in school to interiorize these values. The adults who work as teachers, administrators, and counselors want their students to turn out as decent, hard-working, responsible persons, and they strive with varying degrees of dedication and skill to contribute to wholesome personal development. But it is all too obvious that their success is limited. The incidence of violence, dishonesty, substance abuse, irresponsible sexual activity, and other forms of destructive behavior in and out of school convince many that the schools not only fail to contribute to children's well-being but may even exert a negative influence.

To judge the fairness of these criticisms, one must ask: How realistic are adult expectations? If the schools are indeed failing to fulfill reasonable expectations, why is this so, and what can be done to improve performance?

One of the biggest mistakes one can make is to equate education with schooling. To be sure, education goes on in schools. But children are constantly learning, absorbing messages in the home, on the street, and from the popular entertainment media— recorded music, radio, movies. and television. Many of these messages are freighted with value judgments about what is important, what is valuable, what is worth their attention and energy. And though the home and school may be presumed to be allies most of the time, even their combined educative influence finds a powerful counterpoise in the media. The latter are in many ways more influential than the home or school and in some respects hostile to their shared values. Any serious attempt at making schools more effective in imparting values and forming character must take these countervailing influences seriously and assess their effect on strategies of formal education.

Before analyzing the messages and measuring the influence of popular entertainment, it is necessary to consider the overall cultural context in which the media and schools operate. James Fowler rightly identified the dominant myth of consumer culture: "You should experience everything you desire, own everything you want, and relate intimately with whomever you wish."[1] Many young people accept this view of life. Anyone who tells them that some experiences are wrong or that they have no unrestricted right to sexual intimacy is seen as interfering with their inalienable right to pursue happiness. This implicit philosophy undergirds many people's ideals, judgments, choices, and action. It is expressed and reinforced through the stories and the songs of young and old. The most powerful source of this myth is, of course, commercial advertising, but it is not the only one. The plots of television and movie dramas almost invariably proceed from an affirmation of this philosophy and rarely deviate from the value judgments inherent in it.

Adults who criticize schools or who simply want to improve them should examine their own feelings about the dominant myth of American culture. Parents whose lives exhibit an uncritical acceptance of these priorities should not expect schools to give their children a set of values or moral standards that are in opposition to their own. Since the contradictions are not immediately apparent to all, however, a few classroom stories are in order.

A class of eleventh graders were discussing how to curb unwanted teenage pregnancies, specifically the strategy of dispensing contraceptives in schools. They had just read a counterproposal in which the writer said that it would be better to tell teenagers that sex "is an enriching and serious business between mature people who are emotionally, socially, and even economically able to accept the consequences. . . . Educate them in such things as family values, a healthy and integrated acceptance of sexuality, stability in marital relationships, a sense of obligation toward other persons, and willingness to accept the consequences of one's actions."[2]

One student replied "I feel that this is impossible. The society in which we live is centered around two ideals: sex and money. Sex is used to make money, and money is used to get sex. These values are so instilled in our mind that the plan would not be able to succeed. If our world had more respect for sex, this plan would be great. I find it unfortunate that the world is as it is, but we should try to correct the problem, not run from it with an idea of great moral values."

A university dean, after talking about morality and television with a group of boys and girls in a Brooklyn public school, observed:

> Seemingly, today's television heroes—and heroines—whose immoral behavior is often sumptuously rewarded have become role models for many young Americans. As one young woman noted, Alexis, on "Dynasty," "is bad. Like she's evil. She's vicious and bold and glamorous. And she's everything that any woman would want to be." When I inquired if that included her calculating behavior, the student replied, "Yes, that too. She gets whatever she wants." One of her classmates, speaking of the character J.R. Ewing of "Dallas," added, "I sort of admire the way he can just corrupt everybody and not even let it affect him."[3]

Fighting Back

In the face of these deleterious influences, adults appeal for a renewed emphasis on moral formation. But in this pluralistic society, they do not agree on the kind of morality to be imparted. Pluralism poses its own problems for socialization. To avoid offending anyone, educators have devised one response: value-neutral education. Such teaching tries to inform youngsters about options, encourages interaction and discussion of these options, but studiously refrains from endorsing any one of them for fear of imposing solutions in controversial areas.

Young people need more help than this. They need guidance, role models, and encouragement from committed and caring adults. But to what are adults committed? How deep are

their convictions about what constitutes morally responsible behavior? How firm is the consensus about the so-called basic civic
virtues? Allan Bloom has said that any professor can be sure of
one thing: almost every student entering the university will say
he believes that truth, especially moral truth, is relative.[4] Moreover, the university experience is not likely to challenge this as-
sumption, since moral relativism is a fairly entrenched position
in the world of higher education. Nor is this moral philosophy
limited to academics. Sociologists repeatedly confirm its pervasiveness in the citizenry at large. William McCready of the National Opinion Research Center at the University of Chicago concluded: "Americans don't respond to moral imperatives. They increasingly behave any way they want to. They've been told to
trust their consciences, and that's what they're doing."[5] When
this marks an advance from uncritical reliance on external authority to a search for conviction based on evidence and argument, people are on the road to moral maturity. But the authors
of *Habits of the Heart* indicated that something else is at work
when they explored the underpinnings of this attitude in the
popular mind:

> For many, there is no objectifiable criterion for choosing
> one value or course of action over another. One's own idi-
> osyncratic preferences are their own justification. The right
> act is simply the one that yields the agent the most excit-
> ing challenge or the most good feeling about himself.
>
> In the absence of any objectifiable criteria of right and
> wrong, good or evil. the self and its feelings become our
> only moral guide. But if the individual self must be its
> own source of moral guidance, then each individual must
> always know what he wants and desires or intuit what he
> feels. He must act so as to produce the greatest satisfaction
> of his wants or to express the fullest range of his impulses.
>
> Utility replaces duty: self expression unseats authority.
> "Being good" becomes feeling good.[6]

This perspective shows up in some striking ways in teaching materials used in many schools. Recall Education Secretary

William Bennett's criticism of some of the sex education materials used in public schools. The sex education resources referred to by Bennett give arguments for not engaging in sexual intercourse and try to make students "comfortable" with that decision. His comment is arresting: "You sometimes get the feeling that, for these guides, being 'comfortable' with one's decision, with exercising one's 'option,' is the sum and substance of the responsible life. Decisions aren't right or wrong, decisions simply make you comfortable or not. But American parents expect more than that from their schools. Most Americans want to urge, not what might be the 'comfortable' thing, but the right thing. Why are we so afraid to say what that is?"[7]

Although not all Americans consider morality as residing only in the eye of the beholder, enough of them do to have a significant effect on how not only adults but also young people think about right and wrong. For many people "morality" has come to mean the intrusion of external and coercive authoritarianism. Young people show in a variety of ways that they have absorbed this mentality. They are extremely reluctant to call any behavior "wrong"; the worst label they can apply to the most antisocial actions is "stupid." In their minds, criminals are not evil but "sick." The most heinous atrocities are not wrong but "gross." More than language games are being played here. Ethical judgments become little more than an exercise in aesthetics. But a society that cannot in principle commit itself to basic moral truths has nothing left but a shallow utilitarianism clothed in the shibboleths of "freedom" and "privacy."

When young people engage in destructive behavior in the name of freedom, adults express indignation and call for tighter discipline and control. But their children, aware of the unspoken rules of adult society, see this as a hypocritical enforcement of standards that their elders themselves do not believe in. Adolescents especially resent this seemingly arbitrary imposition. One eleventh grader wrote a reply to a magazine article in which the author argued that the mere distribution of contraceptives in schools was unlikely to decrease the number of teenage pregnancies but might increase it. Completely ignoring the evidence and arguments advanced by the author, the boy responded: "Your stand on contraceptives is really a personal opinion. If parents would allow the contraceptives, teenagers might agree to [sic] their parents because of the willingness of parents to allow freedom of choice. A good family discussion on sex, its true value, contraceptives, and love would give teenagers freedom to make their own decisions without feeling pressured by parents. This is only my opinion, much like, I believe, your article was. You seem to be forcing your opinion on people and that puts a negative tone on things." This peculiar form of self-righteousness reminds one of Bloom's observation: "The inevitable corollary of . . . sexual interest is rebellion against the parental authority that represses it. Selfishness thus becomes indignation and then transforms itself into morality."[8]

A Double Standard

No matter how hard adults try to place reasonable limits on children's freedom and to inculcate standards of responsible behavior, their efforts are likely to fail as long as they are perceived by the young as maintaining a double standard. If privacy is equated with nonaccountability and accepted as the ideal of the moral life, then adolescents will view all moral imperatives as equivalent to the arbitrary limits placed on children. And any attempt by schools to reinforce moral standards will not only be rejected but also resented as an effort to postpone the rewards of maturity and perpetuate childhood.

Young people notice, for example. how adults carry on the debate about that most divisive of issues, abortion. Those who believe in abortion-on-demand do not call themselves "pro-abortion" but "pro-choice." They insist that they are arguing not for abortion but for people's right to choose whether to abort. The unfortunate effect of this kind of argument is to preclude any meaningful dialogue on the question of whether abortion is the unjust taking of human life. The unspoken but inescapable premise of such an argument is that whatever choice one makes is right, so long as it is made freely. Of course, the same people who make this argument forbid their fellow citizens to make free choices to rob, rape, and sell drugs. But no matter. Children hear this nondebate and rightly conclude that adults disagree not about the moral quality of choices but about the right to choose. It does not matter what one does so long as it is done freely. And, of course, one should feel comfortable with it. Anyone who criticizes a choice is at best guilty of bad manners and, at worst, of violating another's privacy.

These observations are bound to enrage many readers and perhaps dissuade them from reading further. But even those who find these ideas uncongenial must admit that in the present climate of opinion it is unrealistic to expect schools to make a meaningful contribution to moral formation. Schools do not operate in a vacuum. The proliferation and refinement of the media make even the least literate of youngsters sensitive to what is going on in the larger society. They sense that the older generation wants to saddle them with a burden of ideals and taboos that even they do not accept. As children see it, the mainsprings of adult behavior are not justice, honesty, and self-discipline but aggression, greed, and self-indulgence This is an overstatement, of course, but it is normal adolescent moralizing, born of disillusionment and fueled by the popular media portrayal of adult motivation. At any rate, the moral crisis among young people seems to be partially a function of the moral confusion and fragmentation in adult society, and the mote in one group's eye can hardly be removed without attending to the beam in the other's.

This should not be interpreted as a counsel of despair. Within the limits imposed by cultural myths, schools can do much to combat the present malaise and assist in children's moral development. At the outset, it must be understood that socialization is a game that must henceforth be played by new rules. In the past, it has meant inducing children to accept the values of adult society. But in a pluralistic, fragmented society lacking consensus in many areas of moral concern, public education must employ more complex strategies. There is a built-in tension in American society between a commitment to individualism and a desire for community. This stress spawns paradoxes like the desire to socialize children without agreeing on the way of life that is considered desirable for them.

The question is: How can schools promote a desirable pluralism without encouraging rootlessness and contributing to fragmentation? How can they encourage tolerance and openness and still avoid lapsing into anomie? This problem lies at the heart of the issue of moral education. Most Americans are deeply committed to freedom of conscience and the preservation of individual liberty. They fear the influence of Moral Majority types and other zealots who would manipulate information, intimidate dissenters, and discourage critical thinking in their single-minded determination to impose a set of values and a way of life. These fears are well grounded. But it is important to understand the roots of the anger in such people. They think that the schools have betrayed their children by creating an amoral, value-free vacuum to be filled by those less responsible vehicles of informal education, television and other media. For all their shortcomings, they understand what many of their adversaries fail to grasp: that freeing children means more than leaving them alone. In their anxiety to fill the vacuum, zealots may undermine the foundation of a free society. But if they are extremists, it is because they are polarized by a society that, they feel, has closed its eyes to their legitimate fears and concerns.

A Third Way

There is a large group of people who receive little publicity but who have the power to break the paralyzing deadlock described above. They perceive the bankruptcy of value-neutral schooling but recoil from the excesses of reactionary indoctrinators. Their existence is barely acknowledged by media analysts who do not know how to fit them into convenient stereotypical categories. They want to exercise responsible authority in the lives of their children and to guide them without stifling initiative or discouraging healthy responsibility and self-determination.

They believe that even the thorniest and most divisive ethical issues are susceptible to reason and dialogue and that children can be taught the skills of moral analysis and decision making. One would be tempted to call them a silent majority if that sobriquet had not been preempted. At any rate, these people are looking for a way out of the present impasse. What can they reasonably expect of their schools by way of moral education?

One thing educators can do is to help children understand the roots of the differences among people. Youngsters are already aware of the differences, but they are a source of confusion until they are addressed in an organized, intentional way. Louis Raths, Merrill Harmin, and Sidney Simon described this confusion and its consequences:

> Being exposed to so many different alternatives, perhaps the child was left with no ideas, but instead absorbed just the confusion. It is possible that the biggest contribution these media made was to baffle the child's nascent understanding of what is right and what is wrong, what is true and what is false, what is good and what is bad, what is just and what is unjust, what is beautiful and what is ugly.

> Out of this welter of traveling and communication, there came not only confusion and uncertainty but also the idea that perhaps anything was all right, nothing really mattered, that while many people were different, there was nothing particularly significant in the differences. One way of life was as good as another. Nobody really was an example of what was the right way to be.[9]

With due attention to the age and ability of students, teachers can help them to discern the unstated premises from which people work, the taken-for-granted worldviews and value systems that underlie choices and life-styles. Young people are capable of this kind of analysis with help from their teachers. They can begin to see that their lives are not necessarily predetermined by forces over which they have no control but can be shaped by conscious, free decisions. They can see how people take different paths, depending on what is more important to them: comfort or achievement, things or people, self-indulgence or service, pleasure or sacrifice, competition or cooperation, egoism or altruism, amorality or integrity. They can begin to grasp the consequences of these choices, how their decisions may affect themselves and society.

This kind of education helps students to answer not only questions like, How can I succeed? but also questions like, What is success? What kind of person do I want to be? What are the sources of life's deepest satisfactions? Here are the wellsprings of personal morality, the sources from which ethical stances derive and moral choices flow. If this sounds too philosophical, that may be due to the drift toward instrumentalism and vocationalism that characterize much education. A 1987 survey of American college freshmen by the American Council on Education and the Higher Education Research Institute found that only 39 percent put great emphasis on developing a meaningful philosophy of life, the lowest proportion in twenty years. This kind of superficiality leaves a vacuum to be filled by the insistent, manipulative messages of consumerism. A record 76 percent of the freshmen said that being financially well-off was a key goal, a number nearly double that of seventeen years before. The survey director concluded: "Despite *Newsweek's* announcement that greed is dead, our data show that it is alive and well. Students still tend to see their life being dependent on affluence and are not inclined to be reflective. Obviously we are seeing something very profound in the society."[10]

What prevents schools from being places of reflection and discussion about values? It is resisted by the well-founded fear of teachers (and, even more, of administrators) that taking positions on moral issues is almost sure to offend those in the community who hold different opinions. According to Raths, Harmin, and Simon: "If someone was for something, someone else was against it; and to avoid controversy, schools began to stand for nothing. Teachers turned toward 'teaching the facts.' In communities of strangers . . . people with many different backgrounds, it became easier to have schools which themselves represented an absence of consensus. Moral, aesthetic values were quietly abandoned as integral parts of the curriculum."[11]

As a result, educators have become skilled at laying out options, delineating choices, and, with studied neutrality, encouraging children to clarify in their own minds what seems important or right to them. Students are prodded not to look for the truth but for what they feel comfortable with. There are no "right" or "wrong" choices, only those that each individual finds agreeable. This can be legitimately termed enlightenment of a sort, but not guidance.

To do better than this, schools would have to attempt something very courageous: they would stand for something. Individual teachers would delineate options and explore the roots of pluralism and controversy with their students. They would encourage critical thinking, stimulate curiosity and questioning, and welcome reasonable disagreement. While respecting the individuality and freedom of students, they would challenge them. Discussion of moral issues would be analytical, rational and respectful. Opinions and people alike would be subject to criticism. But—and most threatening of all—teachers themselves would feel free to agree with some of their students and disagree with others, and to assert their own convictions.

This last proposal will be rejected out of hand, because it threatens the harmony of the school community. Educators have become painfully sensitive to anything that may cause controversy. As it is, harmony has indeed been purchased but at a heavy price. American schools have become bland environments characterized not by the healthy, invigorating clash of opinion and the excitement of discovery but by a deadening dissemination and regurgitation of "facts." They are the last place anyone would go to find out what life is all about. No wonder children are bored. They are taught by people who feel constrained to muffle their deepest convictions about what is right and true and just in the interest of a surface placidity. So, to find out what is really important and how to get it, they turn to the "educators" who have the biggest budgets and the fewest restraints—the hucksters of popular culture. All the evidence indicates that such "teachers" are quite effective and that the children are learning very well indeed, so well that countless parents fear they are losing their children to a way of life that contradicts every important value for which they stand. And then they wonder why their schools do not help to turn the tide.

Taking Risks

The people who run and teach in schools will be understandably nervous about trying the new (old?) approach to education proposed here. Some of them assume that parents *want* schools to be neutral, even mute, in matters of morality and values. Others suspect that forthrightness in such matters will inevitably cause some complaints from adults who object to what is being taught. Ideologues will cry "indoctrination" at the first sign that someone is trying to teach something more than the "facts." In such a climate, people will fear for their jobs, decide that prudence is the better part of valor, and go back to business as usual. But does it have to be this way? Schools can reflect the pluralism of the public not by ignoring the divisions among competing elements but by promoting dialogue, even debate, among them. If America is indeed a free marketplace of ideas, then educators should be permitted not only to display their wares but to promote them.

But suppose students do not share their teachers' opinions. What happens then? Obviously, these views must not be imposed, nor should students be pressured by either overt or subtle sanctions to conform. In any society, no matter how homogeneous, freedom should be respected and encouraged; in a pluralistic one like ours, this should be even more evident. Both parents and students would rightly object to anything smacking of indoctrination. Teachers should aim not at agreement on specific issues but at a shared willingness to pursue standards derived not from an external source but from the young person's own thinking and struggle.

One of the great virtues of our society is respect for diversity. This should not and need not be sacrificed as educators strive to contribute to moral enlightenment and growth. The challenge is to maintain a devotion to searching for the truth without losing regard for those whose search leads to conclusions and commitments in conflict with one's own. Voltaire said it best: "I disapprove of what you say, but I will defend to the death your right to say it." The present state of affairs is unsatisfactory not because the differences among people are accepted but because the roots of these differences are not addressed and hence are regarded as insignificant. The opposite error, no less undesirable, would be to try to obliterate those differences at the price of freedom.

Good teachers know how to steer a middle course between such extremes. Every day, in a variety of subjects, they prod their pupils along the road to learning even as they make allowances for limitations of talent and maturity. Teachers of literature are accustomed to promoting sound interpretation and criticism without stifling independence of thought. They know how to make students feel accepted even when their opinions are not. If these teaching skills could be put to work in the field of moral education, much good could be accomplished.

There are, of course, risks involved in turning schools into centers of ferment rather than leaving them as information sites and skill factories. It is dangerous to let people express, in front of the children, their thoughts and opinions. Feathers will be ruffled, sacred cows will be gored, parent-teacher sessions may go on longer, and school-board meetings could even suffer a diminution of civility. But these signs may not portend destruction but stirrings of life.

The alternative would be the status quo. In their headlong rush to the shelter of neutrality, schools have unwittingly become havens of the unexamined life. In their anxiety to offend no one, they have become eunuchs incapable of impregnating their students with anything remotely resembling a passion for truth. But they are not harmless, either. While the hypocritical tastemakers of mass culture hide behind First Amendment fortifications and conduct their hard-sell assault on the minds and hearts of the young, those who are supposed to be allies of parents are mute. All this reminds one of Edmund Burke's famous aphorism: "The only thing necessary for the triumph of evil is for good men to do nothing." It is not a question of choosing between danger and safety, but of deciding which dangers to confront.

Some will interpret this as an assault on liberalism. But there is a difference between liberal education and the education of liberals. Liberal education steers a middle path between the extremes of value-free schooling and indoctrination and tries to help students choose their lives. It recognizes that the young will never find their way through the maze of ignorance and self-deception without coming into vital, even abrasive contact with caring adults who demonstrate their own commitment to honesty, truth, and justice. It is not even important that these adults believe or say the same things; indeed, it is probably not desirable. It is important that they clearly stand for something more than self-aggrandizement and infect their students not necessarily with their own beliefs but with their devotion to the search for enlightenment and righteousness.

There are certainly schools where good things happen, where teachers do more than transmit information and skills, where they challenge and inspire young people. Moral education takes many forms, from the English class where literature is a springboard for serious reflection to the history class that grapples with social issues, to the adults who simply demand honesty and settle for nothing less from anyone, beginning with themselves. But these are bright spots on a drab landscape and will remain so as long as schools reflect a society muddled in its thinking, unsure of what it believes, and protective only of a lonely individualism. A community fragmented in its values and commitments should not be scandalized when its schools do little more than mirror its own divisions and uncertainties.

Educators do not have to be uncertain trumpets, and many of them are more than that, but it takes an unusual store of moral conviction and courage to rise above the general level of mediocrity. In the present moral climate, where teachers march to many different drummers, a clear and firm note of moral leadership is bound to be a bit of a surprise.

Topics for Discussion

1. Do you know of any public schools where effective moral education goes on?

2. Do you agree that "the older generation wants to saddle youth with a burden of ideals and taboos that even they do not accept"?

3. How can public schools avoid becoming havens of the unexamined life?

Endnotes

1. James Fowler, *Stages of Faith* (New York: Harper & Row, 1981), 20.

2. Joseph Bernardin, "Abortion and Teenage Pregnancy," *New York Times*, 22 Jan. 1978.

3. Herbert London, "What TV Drama is Teaching Our Children," *New York Times*, 23 Aug. 1987.

4. Allan Bloom, *The Closing of the American Mind* (New York: Simon & Schuster, 1987), 73-74.

5. Kenneth Briggs, "Religious Feeling Seen Strong in U.S.," *New York Times*, 9 Dec. 1984.

6. Robert Bellah et al., *Habits of the Heart* (New York: Harper & Row, 1985), 75-76.

7. "Sex and the Education of Our Children," *America*, 14 Feb. 1987, 122.

8. Bloom, 74.

9. Louis Raths, Merrill Harmin, and Sidney Simon, *Values and Teaching* (Columbus, Ohio: Charles F. Merrill Publishing Co., 1966), 17-18.

10. Deidre Carmody, "To Freshmen, A Big Goal is Wealth," *New York Times*, 14 Jan. 1988.

11. Raths, Harmin, and Simon, 20.

Chapter 11

Everything You Didn't Want to Know About Sex

MOST TEENS WOULD AGREE THAT ADULTS WORRY TOO MUCH. Especially parents. Especially about sex.

A class of high school juniors, when asked to offer advice to parents of other teens, came up with these messages:

- Most parents today are scared witless about discussing sex. Their attitudes are very puritanical and archaic.

- Parents shouldn't force their values on their children. They should be open and receptive to their children's sexual problems.

- Tell the parents that their children love them very much, and that they appreciate their concern for their safety. Most teenagers agree that haphazard premarital sex is wrong, but, in cases where there is an intimate relationship, sex is a beautiful thing and can be engaged in, even though there may be consequences.

But parents persist in worrying, especially when they think about the "consequences." They know that over a million unmarried teenage girls in this country get pregnant each year. They know that, of all the girls who are presently 14 years old, two out of five will be pregnant by age 19. They worry about the abortions, about the unwise teen marriages contracted under pressure, about venereal disease, and about AIDS. They tend to agree with the author of a recent magazine article who wrote: "Teenagers are not ready for sexual intercourse because they are not ready for its psychological, emotional, spiritual, and biological consequences."

An eleventh grade boy answered the article this way:

> A famous American once said, "No guts, no glory." When one doesn't know what lies ahead, he should try to find out. Like advancing on a hill in battle or starting a business, one can make estimates about sexual intercourse, but can't really know what it is like until he tries. Protection of man's inalienable right to pursue happiness has made this country great. You can say that "teenagers are not ready for sexual intercourse because they are not ready for its psychological, emotional, spiritual, and biological consequences," but there will always be teenagers who can prove you wrong.

Like many young people, he cannot imagine bad things happening to *him*—it's always about other kids who are not as smart or as careful or as lucky as he is. To persons of his mentality, anyone who suggests limits is interfering with his inalienable right to pursue happiness. Supporting this naiveté is the adolescent myth of invincibility. That is one reason why adult warnings about pregnancy or sexually transmitted diseases are dismissed by most youngsters as "scare tactics." As Alfred E. Newman would say, "What, me worry?"

Of course, there are many other factors involved, too. A 17-year-old boy writes:

> Peer pressure at this time is tremendous. You want to be accepted as sexually normal. If your friends have a more exciting social life than you do, some people will accuse

you of homosexuality. These accusations can have a horrible effect on your life. Rumors do not stop easily; they can destroy someone.

When you date a girl, the peer group tells you to push, go as far as you can. They expect a good story. In their eyes, a girl is a toy you use for fun and status. They don't care about her as a person at all. Often the ideal is to "love them and leave them."

Experiences like these make it look as if some teenage sexual activity doesn't have much to do with the pursuit of happiness, and even less with love or affection. One older student told a youth minister that he never had sex with a girl more than once because he was not ready to establish deep relationships. Another fellow admitted that while he had sex with girls, he never told any of them that he loved them or cared about them because he didn't want to get involved in a serious relationship.

Unlike those who talk about the weather but do nothing about it, those who are concerned about the alarming rise in teen-age pregnancies and abortions are determined to do something about it. Most agree that some kind of sex education is needed, but they cannot agree on what kind. Should it stress family values and self-discipline, or should it go the pragmatic route and dispense contraceptive information and materials? To those on both sides of this acrimonious debate, and to those who have not made up their minds, I offer some observations and suggestions in the hope that effective help may come to our growing children before it is too late.

Any doctor knows that good prescription and treatment depend on careful, accurate diagnosis. An examination of adolescents that takes into account certain psychological and sociological data may help us to avoid dispensing cures that either fail to address the disease or threaten to make it worse. And it may point the way toward strategies that will help real young people and not the ones that exist only in our dull, adult minds.

Pressure and Fear

Young people have always been inclined to go for too much sex too soon, but their problems today are qualitatively different from those of earlier generations. They are under tremendous pressure to perform, to prove their sexual adequacy, not only to their peers, but to themselves. The fear of homosexuality is there, but even stronger is the fear of being accused of it. In some circles it does not take much to incur this charge. The sexually inactive are presumed guilty until proved "innocent" in a reversal of that term's meaning that is as revealing as it is ironic. There are other fears, too—of being sheltered, of missing out, of being left behind by peers. And then there are the insistent messages of television sitcoms, movies and rock music lyrics: "Hey, everybody's doing it, it's no problem, why aren't you?" In the present climate, reservations become "hang-ups." Adolescents have enough trouble developing a positive self-image and feelings of competence even in the best of times. As a group, they are very vulnerable to such pressures and often too inexperienced to perceive the shallowness of the implicit argument that experience guarantees maturity.

It is hard to exaggerate the impact of the media upon the young. Seldom do the media portray sexuality as linked with commitment, stable family relationships and child-bearing. Instead, it is associated with romance, with casual encounters or temporary relationships, with the unspoken premise that fidelity or permanence are not to be expected and may even be undesirable. On the silver screen and the boob tube, James Bond and other sexual athletes go through disposable women who make no demands beyond the moment, who never get pregnant—or at least never worry about it. Men and women move in and out of intimate relationships with no apparent damage. And, of course, marriage vows count for nothing. In short, "all you need is love." But teen-agers are hard pressed to tell the differences among desire, infatuation and love or to see ahead to the consequences that follow on miscalculation. One 16-year-old boy in my class wrote: "I'm pretty sure that if parents were really sure that the

kids were as in love as they say they were, they'd be more ac-
cepting of their kids having sex. If you're really in love, there is
nothing wrong with sex."

But it is not just the inexperience and the naivete of young
people that put them at risk. Underlying the images and the
media messages is what James Fowler calls the dominant myth
of consumer society: You should own all you can, experience
whatever you desire and relate intimately with whomever you
wish. If a young person or an adult has consciously or unconsciously bought into this myth and the values and life style that
go with it, exhortations to discipline or self-control fall on deaf
ears. Herein lies the attractiveness of the contraceptive strategy.
It is purely pragmatic, utterly practical and leaves unchallenged
a whole way of looking at life and love and sex. The contraceptive distributors accept this philosophy without question.
They unconsciously insult our children by telling them, in effect,
that not only is there nothing better, but that they are not capable
of it, anyway. And then they claim to show them how to have
sex without consequences. But as Cardinal Joseph L. Bernardin of
Chicago has pointed out, there is no such thing as sex without
consequences—and these go far beyond unwanted pregnancy.

Not Just a Youth Problem

It must be clear by now that we are talking not just about
the sexual problems of youth, but of grown-ups as well. Adolescents rightly see adult society as hypocritical when their elders
accept the dominant culture's myths without question, live by
them in their own lives and then slap their children's hands
when they reach for a share of the forbidden fruit. Just as the
abortion problem will never be solved until society at large
changes its ways of judging and treating pregnant women, so the
crisis of mass teen-age pregnancy cannot be effectively addressed
without a radical shift in adult values, attitudes and behavior
with regard to sex. Neither contraceptive strategies nor traditional moral approaches are going to cut any ice with the young

as long as adults persist in treating this as a youth problem and try to take the mote out of adolescents' eyes while leaving the beam in their own.

Since such a counterrevolution is a long way off, we have to live in the present and help our children here and now. Where do we begin? Whenever we try to convert people, we should start where people are and, if possible, with shared ideas and values. For example, we need to ask such questions as: What are the motives of young people who jump into bed before they are ready? What are they looking for? Is there a shared language of concern possible between them and us?

Indeed, there is. Although teen-age pregnancies and other sexual problems sometimes occur in casual, recreational contexts, the boy quoted earlier was correct when he said that most teen-agers disapprove of haphazard or promiscuous sex. They believe that intimacy is justified only by love, though they often mistake infatuation for love. As another teen-ager told me, "I think that parents today have no concept of how truly close two young people can be. . . . Parents just don't think it's possible for a guy and a girl to be deeply committed to each other."

Several girls spoke in the same vein about commitment:

> Premarital sex is wrong if you do not love the person, but if you are willing to take responsibility for your actions and are committed in some way to the person, it is all right.

> Two people should be committed to each other before they have sex. But commitment does not have to mean marriage. Just because two people aren't married does not mean that they are not committed to each other forever.

Notice the way they use the word "committed." We have often heard adolescents assert that intercourse is all right for unmarried people, including teen-agers, so long as they are "committed" to each other. (Many adults, too, speak this way.) When one pursues this notion with them, it becomes clear that there is no content to the word, that it has changed meaning. What it means, in effect, is: "I like you a lot, and I wouldn't want you to get hurt." What is implied, but left unsaid, is: "I will be with you as long as I feel this way." But there are no concrete or long-term obligations. We have come a long way from "for richer for poorer, for better for worse, in sickness and in health, till death do us part." When words like these change their meaning, they point to something significant that is happening to people who use the words. Adolescence, of course, is not a time for long-term commitments, deep attachments, stable relationships. It is a time for discovery, for experimentation, for trying on identities. Relationships of teen-age boys and girls can indeed be warm and affectionate and can be sources of genuine growth, so long as not too much is invested in them. But when they are confused with love, given the false name of commitment and perceived as justifying total intimacy, confusion ensues, mistakes are made and wounds inflicted that do not always heal.

Adolescents can, with a little help, see truths like these. They do not want to be told that sex is "bad," and they want to be taken seriously. They yearn for affirmation, for friendship, for intimacy. They are intensely interested in relationships and want to know how to evaluate them. They want to develop the skills needed to relate to others, especially those of the opposite sex. They are, for all their sophistication, quite innocent and uninformed about some very basic matters. The distinction between love and infatuation, the first time they hear it, comes as a revelation. They are usually quite uninformed about the quality and the meaning of sexual experience and response on the part of the opposite sex, and hence misread the signals they give to one another, sometimes with tragic consequences. They need to formulate for themselves a set of standards, a sexual morality, not imposed from above and accepted uncritically, but based on their own values and felt needs, on their best and most generous instincts. But they cannot do it alone or without help from wise and caring adults who can share their world of ideas and concerns and lead them through the thickets of propaganda and half-truths that surround them. This is what real sex education is all about, not the threats of puritanical zealots nor the well-meaning but shoddy tactics of the promoters of contraception.

In advocating this kind of sex education we are not excluding warnings against pregnancy and venereal disease. This kind of motivation is more relevant than ever. But parents and other sex educators need more arguments than these. Their children need to know, not only the dangers involved in irresponsible sexual activity, but also what attitudes and behavior go into the making of fulfilling, rewarding sex. What are the qualities of mature, loving, stable relationships? How does one become a good lover—not a stud or a sexpot, but a wife or husband, a mother or father? What are the characteristics of a marriage relationship that is happy and growing? How does a young man or woman develop such qualities as warmth, communication, responsiveness, fidelity, caring, unselfishness? These are what love is all about. Young people need to be told that such qualities do not come wrapped up with the wedding presents. They must be learned and cultivated during youth and throughout young adulthood. They are not learned by practicing exploitiveness, dishonesty, casual intimacy and insensitivity. We must not treat one another like throw-away items. As one wise 17-year-old observed, "People are not toys; you cannot play with them and put them away." Here, in considerations like these, are the building blocks of a sexual code that young people can believe in and aspire to.

A host of objections will no doubt be brought against this kind of approach to teen-agers. The ethical and religious illiterates will accuse us of imposing some sectarian ideology. To this mentality, as Robert Bellah and his associates have pointed out in *Habits of the Heart:* "Any intrusion of 'oughts' and 'shoulds' into relationships is rejected as an intrusion of external and coercive authoritarianism."

More thoughtful skeptics will wonder if it is too idealistic, asking more of immature youngsters than they can deliver. They deserve a serious answer. Youth, we must remember, is a time of life ripe for idealism. Most teen-agers want to do what is right. They want to be responsible, caring people capable of love and intimacy. They can understand that loving is more than a technique, and can be shown that it is more than a feeling. They are capable of grasping the insight that love is a project, an enterprise that demands the best of us and, like anything worthwhile, may cost effort and sacrifice. If the taste-makers who turn out the spiritual junk food that passes for entertainment do not talk about sex this way, does that forbid us to do so? And dare we presume that the young will not listen, if we have not tried?

This kind of sex education is not just a gee-whizzy, upbeat, sanitized view of reality. It involves helping young people to be honest with themselves and with one another, to appraise their own behavior at its worst as well as its best. It means exposing selfishness, duplicity and all the other games that young and not-so-young people play when sex is involved. It spells out the other consequences of irresponsible sex that Cardinal Bernardin alluded to: the self-centeredness, the desensitizing, the cynicism and distrust that it brings in its wake. As Richard Hettlinger once remarked, people who are lucky or careful or both and manage to avoid unwanted pregnancies can get hurt in many other ways. Their capacity for meaningful, loving relationships can be eroded very early in life.

Troubled Families

Another factor that makes the Christian vision of sex hard to accept is the negative experiences that many young people encounter in troubled families. Divorce and separation have touched many of them, and some of the families that stay together are not happy ones. It is all too easy for them to conclude that marriage and family life are not worth the effort. It's an easy next step to rationalize all kinds of compromises—living together without marriage, moving from relationship to relationship without any real commitment, or just plain recreational sex without regard for those they use.

Finally, there is the most common illusion of all—that they can have it both ways. According to this compromise, they don't reject the goal of marriage and family life, they just postpone it to that distant time when they're ready to "settle down." Until then, they play at love, enjoy intimacy, and speak the language of commitment while avoiding the reality. They think they can move from fun sex to more serious but temporary relationships and then emerge from these adventures ready to give one person all they have, with no reservations, for better or for worse, 'til death do them part.

Of course it doesn't work. That's why so many marriages are doomed from the start. After years of one kind of behavior, people are expected to make 180-degree turns and change totally their ways of relating to persons of the opposite sex. After years of telling little lies and hanging loose and breaking promises and using people, they expect to be transformed, on their wedding day, into spouses capable of total honesty, genuine commitment, fidelity, and dependability.

Young people can understand this kind of straight talk and they have a right to hear it. True, the children of fractured families may find it harder to relate to all of this and see it as an attainable goal. But we can only respond, in the words of the great philosopher Howard Cosell, that one must tell it like it is. And meanwhile, in an imperfect world, those primary sexual educators called parents must do their very best, in their own families, to be living evidence that people can indeed live that way some of the time and aspire to it the rest of the time.

We cannot leave the subject of parents without one more observation about their role in sex education. The greatest gift parents can give their children is unconditional love, the kind that is based not on the child's achievements or talents or anything else and which will survive any disappointment. The young person who is loved like this and knows herself or himself to be so loved is much less likely to go after the counterfeit forms of love offered by premature sexual intimacy. Children of warm, stable families who experience affection and perceive themselves as unconditionally loved are much less likely to settle for substitutes when they know they have the real thing, and when the people closest to them show by their very lives what sex and love are really all about.

Have we forgotten someone? Does God have anything to do with all this? The answer is "yes," to be sure. But the kind of sex education that we have been proposing can be implemented by all people of good will, by people of any religion and maybe by those with no religion. But while not explicitly religious, the views expressed here come out of a world view best described as Judeo-Christian. They presuppose a creation that is good, graced by a God who calls us to love one another the way Jesus Christ has loved us—unselfishly and without reserve. We believe that God wants us to aim high, and that more than sufficient grace is available for us. The ideals expressed here are not attainable by purely human resources; they are proposed to us by one who tells us to be perfect as His heavenly Father is perfect. Our actions tell our children much more about this God than do our words. But if we do speak to them about God when we talk about sex, let us tell them not about One who makes arbitrary demands, but about a loving Father who reminds us of what reality itself requires, and that when these demands seem beyond our strength, we can do all things in God who strengthens us.

The national crisis of teen-age pregnancies is one for which there is no quick fix. This bitter fruit of the sexual revolution has been a long time coming. It has claimed adolescents as its most visible casualties, but not the only ones. The way back to a sexually healthy and responsible society will be long and painful. But we can make a start with our children by exposing, for what it is, a way of life that has betrayed both young and old, and then pointing the way to a better one. If we are capable of this kind of humility and honesty with our teen-age children, they may pay us back with the most precious thing that youth has to give: hope.

Topics for Discussion

1. Do you think we can make a convincing case against teenage premarital sex without insisting on extramarital chastity among adults? Or are they two different issues?

2. How would you explain to an adolescent the differences among physical desire, infatuation, and love?

3. Do you think that young people people can, with adult help, "formulate for themselves a sexual morality not imposed from above but based on their own values and felt needs, on their best and most generous instincts"?

Chapter 12

The Educator as Minister

Okay, but whose job is it?

Even those who agree with most of the ideas in this book may well wonder who bears the responsibility for this day-to-day work of handing on a religious tradition and contributing to the moral development of students in Catholic schools.

The answer, in one word, is: Everybody. Every adult involved in education is, by that very fact, called to Christian ministry.

This may seem like too sweeping a statement.

The notion of teachers in Catholic high schools being ministers may seem like a new idea, but it is really an old one. Until about thirty years ago, teachers and other staff members saw themselves as part of an institution promoting religious socialization and development. In that not-so-distant past everyone "taught religion" by hearing students' recitation of catechism. This practice still persists in many Catholic grammar schools where every teacher is expected to take a turn teaching religion.

Then with the Second Vatican Council and its aftermath, specialization arrived. As the religion teacher's task became more difficult, it required special training and qualifications. The catechism went the way of the dinosaur.

Now teachers of "secular" subjects don't see where they fit in. They often perceive religious and moral formation as the private preserve of the chaplain and the religion department. The trouble with this arrangement is that now it is all too clear that the specialists cannot do it all. If our schools are to be anything more than vehicles for the upward mobility of baptized pagans, the entire staff must contribute to the creation of a genuine Christian environment. But how?

If you are an administrator or if you teach subjects other than religion, here are some ways you can contribute to a school's being Christian in more than name.

First and probably most important of all, be a good teacher or administrator. There is no substitute for competence; that's basic justice. Consider your position not as "just a job" but as a professional calling. Take a personal interest in your students and your colleagues.

If you are more than an educated hack or scholarly functionary, you will be sensitive to "value situations" in which people's rights or feelings, as well as tasks or marks, are at stake. Be aware of justice issues, especially when honesty or racism is involved. (Administrators have a special responsibility here.) Speak out. Don't look the other way when people are abused or taunted or manipulated. Take a stand. Children often interpret as approval adult silence in the face of injustice.

If your field is social studies or English, do you view yourself as one who teaches a "value-free" subject? Do you unwittingly contribute to the amorality of many young people's approach to life by an "objective," nonjudgmental approach to social and moral issues? Do you see yourself as simply a purveyor of information and imparter of skills, or do you feel any responsibility for the values your students espouse? Does it matter to you what they believe in? Are your students aware that you want them to be anything besides academic successes?

In a church-related school, many opportunities arise for your students to see you not only as a competent teacher or efficient administrator but as a committed Christian. Join in worship and prayer with the school community. Show support for reconciliation services. Help with retreats and days of recollection when the opportunity is offered. If you cannot be personally involved, give active and explicit encouragement to these important religious experiences. If services and outreach programs need help, try to pitch in.

Do You Care?

Not everyone can do all these things, which sometimes demand time and energy that may be in short supply. But everyone can do something. To do any of them, you have to really care about the students' moral and spiritual growth. Do you?

While we're examining our consciences, here's one for administrators: Who get rewarded and recognized at your school? We can probably take it for granted that academic excellence is publicly praised, that athletic teams hear the cheers, and that extracurricular activities get publicized. Do those engaged in volunteer community service and charitable projects receive comparable affirmation and recognition? Are there prizes for the most unselfish as well as for the smartest and the best coordinated? And if there aren't, what does this say to your students about the *operative*—and not just the professed—values of the school?

Still, many wonder if this trip is necessary. Why can't the religion department and the chaplain take care of religious learning and practice while the other teachers stick to their subjects and administrators stick to administration? This is an honest objection and a serious one, and it needs to be answered if the great majority of educators are to see their calling as ministers and respond with commitment.

To realize why it is so important for a whole school staff to think and feel and act like ministers, you must understand the peculiar sociological context in which Christian schools operate in today's society. If the dominant culture were permeated by religious sensibility and Christian concerns, then our schools would resonate with that culture and reinforce its values. In such a world, our children would encounter the process of socialization as a unified experience.

But of course the world is nothing like that. From television, music, movies, peers, and even from home, our students are taught the importance of winning, grabbing, accumulating, consuming, and enjoying in a materialistic and hedonistic vacuum. In church and chapel and religion class, they are taught the worth of unselfishness, service, sharing, compassion, honesty, and integrity. Can you blame the kids if they sometimes look on religion as having nothing to do with the real world?

Christian schools are supposed to offer an alternative vision of life, of what it means to be a successful human being. Often they do. But how is such a vision to be credible? In the face of massive psychological pressures emanating from so many facets of society, how can young people shut out the siren call to a plastic paradise and aspire to the demanding ideals of Christianity? Do you realize how different from their contemporaries we are asking them to be?

Wanted: Models

If young people are to respond positively and generously to this alternative vision, they need more than good religion courses and well-planned liturgies and inspiring retreats. They need adult models with whom they can identify, whom they look up to, who demonstrate daily by deed and word that Christian living is both possible and rewarding. They need to be around grown-ups who are neither greedy nor selfish nor exploitive and yet are happy and at peace with themselves and with one another. It's nice when chaplains and religious men and women fill that description, but it's also expected of them. It's even better when married and single, older and younger lay persons who are neither professed religious nor teach religion give this kind of example. This is the stuff of which credibility is made. This is ministry.

Most of our students do not come to our schools to get an alternative vision of life. They come because they've heard that we're "a good school." For some young people this includes religious and moral elements, but for many it simply means a leg up on the ladder of material success. Often their parents' perspective is just as narrow. Their picture of what we are about is not so much distorted as it is incomplete. We do take seriously our responsibility to strive for academic achievement and to provide the learning and the skills needed to survive and prosper in a competitive society. If we do less than that, we have no right to call ourselves a Christian school.

Those of us who are trying to make our schools Christian in fact as well as in name face a formidable task. The opposition comes not only from outside, from a surrounding culture that in so many ways is hostile to the values we espouse. Opposition also comes from within, in as many as four ways.

First, many parents have no interest in the religious and moral dimensions of education, and they are simply using us as vehicles of upward mobility. Second, many students come to us so imbued with contrary values and aspirations and behavior patterns that they turn off whatever threatens their actual or hoped-for lifestyle. Third, the structures of recognition, reward, and discipline—what Lawrence Kohlberg calls the school's "hidden agenda"—sometimes contradict and undermine the values we profess. And finally, staff members can unconsciously throw sand in the wheels, sometimes by cynicism, more often by apathy. As Eldridge Cleaver said, "If you're not part of the solution, you're part of the problem."

If everything we have said in this chapter leaves you unmoved—if you still "just want to teach your subject" and not concern yourself with the Christian formation of your students—then they know it. And you *are* influencing them, whether you know it or not.

If you do care about something more than marks and college board scores, and if you wonder if your contribution to the school can be characterized as genuine ministry, try this wild scenario: Imagine that the Communists have seized power and are trying to root out all vestiges of organized religion. The Red Guards come to your school one day. They call upon the students to identify those teachers and administrators who are known to practice religion or who have tried to infect them with the superstition known as Christianity. If atheism is to triumph, they must be the first to go. Supposing that the kids have been effectively brainwashed, who do you suppose would be turned in? Whoever they are, they're the ones whose educational effects have amounted to ministry.

How about you? Are you on the list? Or are you safe?

Topics for Discussion

1. Do the professed and operative values of your school coincide?

2. Does your school consciously and perceptibly offer an alternative vision of life? How?

3. Many school staff members engage in ministry without realizing it. Do you see this happening? How?

Chapter 13

Ministering to the Young

OPEN THE HIGH-SCHOOL CLASSROOM DOOR A CRACK AND LISTEN TO the following exchange between a teacher and a student. They are considering a hypothetical moral dilemma.

TEACHER: . . . So those are the choices open to her. What should she do?

STUDENT: It's up to her.

TEACHER: Yes, I know it's up to her. So what should she do?

STUDENT: It's her choice.

TEACHER: *[Taking a deep breath to avoid losing his temper]*
Yes, we know it's her choice. But how should she choose? And on what grounds?

STUDENT: It's her choice.

As a high-school religion teacher, I have engaged in this kind of non-conversation many times in recent years. This is not, however, a plea for sympathy. It is my contention that this little bit of theater of the absurd carries an important message for all who minister to the young. In these concluding pages you will hear many of these young people speaking and writing in their own words about religious and moral concerns. They are boys and girls, urban and suburban, ranging from freshmen to seniors, coming from various parts of the country. Some are from Catholic schools, others from public institutions. Their attitudes toward God, church, faith and justice vary widely, as does their receptivity to religious experience. Listening to them, see if you hear in the background the voices of their elders, and maybe a bit of yourself. You may conclude, as I have, that most of them are rich in promise and hungry for enrichment, but that they daily encounter formidable obstacles.

Those of us who have dedicated ourselves to youth ministry have chosen work which is always difficult, sometimes frustrating, usually thankless, and occasionally exhilarating. We persist in our calling out of love for our young people, convinced that we are sowing seeds for the future church. Twenty years from now our students and retreatants and members of our parish youth groups will help determine the shape of the American Church. Will it be predominantly a Church of disciples or of religious consumers? Disciples are Church members whose basic beliefs, values, priorities, commitments, and conduct are shaped by the Gospel message. Religious consumers use religion as a product, to be purchased only when the need arises to provide such items as christenings, weddings, funerals, and safe schools for their children. It has at most a marginal impact on the direction and conduct of their lives.

Traditionally, youth is a source of rejuvenation for any society. Members of the younger generation bring energy, enthusiasm, idealism, and openness to new ideas, perspectives, and challenges. To tap into these resources of Catholic youth, religious leaders will have to address certain issues and overcome certain obstacles in American life today. Failure to do so will result in a Church of religious consumers, lacking vitality, commitment, and the faith that does justice.

Issues and Obstacles

What we have already said about these issues and obstacles earlier in this book should have made it clear that they are by no means the private preserve of youth. At last report, apples were still not falling far from trees. The behavior of young people, in religion as in other areas of life, has a way of reflecting the prejudices and preoccupations of their elders. Because they are usually more blunt and up-front in their words and actions and less skilled than adults in masking their attitudes and motivations, they tend to reveal certain social trends in stark and arresting ways.

If we ignore them and treat them as undeserving of our attention, we miss a chance to understand what is really going on in the minds and hearts not only of the young but also of the not-so-young. We run the risk of turning our backs on the future. We will have preserved our complacency, but at the price of being irrelevant to a whole emerging generation. On the other hand, if we listen to young people and take them seriously, we may enhance our ability to understand, communicate with, and influence them for good both now and in their adult years.

What are these issues and obstacles that affect the religious and moral formation of the young? Without pretending that our list is exhaustive, let us consider these five:

1. An unfriendly dominant culture

2. Individualism

3. Inadequate images of God and Jesus

4. Notions of morality

5. Understandings of religion

An Unfriendly Dominant Culture

It requires no great insight to see that, as a way of life, Christianity is becoming increasingly counter-cultural in today's society. The dominant culture of consumerism defines the human person in terms of the acquisition and consumption of material goods. It promotes the values of getting, owning, enjoying, producing, competing, and winning, all of which emphasize aggressiveness, self-satisfaction, status, and security. As George Aschenbrenner has pointed out, possessions, power, pleasure, and prestige are morally neutral until one perceives them no longer as adornments of the self but as constituting one's very identity. As the Cadillac ad said a few years ago, "You are what you drive."

Over against this worldview stand certain basic Christian convictions. The worth of a person cannot be measured by the money or the things that he or she owns. Frugality is to be preferred to conspicuous consumption. We are responsible for one another. Justice and honesty are not to be compromised in the struggle for status and security. This is different from a kind of economic puritanism which sees wealth and affluence as somehow obscene in themselves. But Christianity relativizes every good except God and insists with St. Augustine that our hearts will be restless as long as they rest in anything less.

The youth of America are restless, all right, but not that way.

Recall the 1987 survey of incoming college freshmen, which showed that from 1966 to 1988 the number of students who thought that developing a meaningful philosophy of life was an essential or very important goal dropped from 83% to 39%.[1] To which one of my high school students replied: "The way the world is now, being well off should be an important thing. A meaningful philosophy of life cannot help you in the real world."

Another boy reflected,

Everyone is concerned with monetary gains, their main motivation throughout life. We all (that is, most of us) have one basic goal in life: "to look good, eat good, and smell good." For instance, take the students in this school. Don't believe the bull they tell you, that they chose to come to this school because "I'll be better able to execute my role as a Christian," or some other pious statement. They chose to come here because it will be a gold star on their record, which in turn will get them into a good college, which in turn will get them into a high-paying job.

But if existential questions are uninteresting, and reflectiveness is discouraged, and a meaningful philosophy of life cannot help you in the "real world," what happens to religion? It cannot make you look good or smell good either. To *feel* good, maybe? We shall see.

Religion is not the only casualty of this mentality. A character in a Billy Joel song, "Angry Young Man," says that he has outgrown idealism and social awareness. He no longer believes in causes, and he has renounced all activism on behalf of justice. Convinced that taking moral stands has no effect on real life, he has decided to look out only for his own survival.

Some eleventh-graders had these reactions:

> Although I can see what those who protest against injustice are saying and I sympathize and identify with them as well, as far as practical and *sensible* considerations go, I think Joel has the upper hand. Results make more concrete sense than abstract feelings.

> In a serious situation, I would hope that I would act in a principled manner. However, as I get older and have more to lose, I think I will "harden" and start looking to survive as best I can.

> I think Billy Joel is a lot like me. There are a few people of conscience who care about others, but most people are just out for Number One, and I presume that I will become like them. For I must get all I can.

Not everyone in the group agreed. Two expressed themselves quite differently:

> I can't see how someone could keep repressing his feelings and not fighting for what he believes is right. That kind of person might as well not even bother to exist.

> If I think something is wrong, I'm going to say something about it even if I know it is not going to change things. I will go to my grave at least knowing I tried to act according to my principles.

Where do young people learn these lessons and find out how to behave in the real world? Mostly, it would seem, from the mass media. One of the most powerful educational tools is advertising. As Jean Kilbourne has observed, advertisements influence our attitudes, and attitudes shape and determine our behavior. Advertising is the propaganda of consumer culture. It tells us that we should be consumers, that happiness can be bought, and that products can fulfill us and meet our deepest human needs.[2] Commenting on the underlying theme of television commercials, Erich Fromm said, "It is the general fear of not being loved, and then to be able, by some product, to be loved."[3]

Underlying these images and messages is what Fowler has earlier described as consumer culture's dominant myth: You should experience whatever you desire, own whatever you want, and relate intimately with whomever you wish. It takes no imagination to see that, to the extent that people young or old uncritically interiorize such a myth, they severely compromise their capacity for religious or moral integrity.

What can the youth minister do in the face of a pervasive culture that is hostile to moral and religious values? One overall strategy is to help young people to engage in a sophisticated critical analysis of the dominant culture, its media and messages, and then explicitly to present Christianity as an alternative vision of life.

Time and again, in ways explicit and implicit, I remind my students that they are *free*—that no one, neither God nor Church nor school, can make them be or do anything they don't want to do or be. In a few years even their parents will lose any control over them. They have the power to choose their lives. They can be generous or selfish; they can choose careers that serve or that just use other people; they can aspire to a fully human life, or they can settle for conspicuous consumption; they can be sexually responsible or irresponsible. It's a free country, and they can choose any of these paths that they desire.

I tell them I don't want to hear any complaints like "The Church won't let us do such and such." Short of breaking the civil law, you can do anything you please, and the Church can't do a thing about it. So grow up. Stop grumbling and passing the buck. Take responsibility for your choices. Choose your life.

What's that? You're not sure what you want to be? Okay, let's talk. No, I'm not going to tell you what to do with your life. If I did, you wouldn't listen anyway. But let's look at the different ways people live. How they make their money and what they spend it on. How they relate to other people. What they consider important. How they think about the purpose of life, about God, about right and wrong. Where and how they look for happiness, and whether or not they find it, and how you can tell.

This exploration takes us down some familiar paths, which we may now see in a wholly new way. My students and I look at the life-styles, not only of the rich and famous, but of all the people who are trying to get that way, including most of us. We examine the taken-for-granted assumptions with which people start but which they rarely reflect upon. These are found mostly in the messages of popular culture as expressed in stories, songs, entertainment—most of all in advertising. They are usually implicit and have to be brought to consciousness by critical analysis.

We also look at other, competing philosophies of life, including Christianity. Beneath the Church practices and customs and rules and popular stereotypes, what is the value system which Jesus and his followers take as their starting point? Does Christ's way of looking at the world make sense? Would living by his principles be likely to bring us satisfaction and fulfillment? What is the price tag on his way of life? What is the cost of discipleship? How does it compare with the program of the dominant culture? What happens when people accept his worldview, embrace his ideals, and try to live by them? Would I want to try?

There are some good precedents for this approach. In ancient Rome, catechumens were informed quite clearly that they had to choose between two irreconcilable ways of life. Jesus himself tells us that we cannot serve two masters, and that, before we set out to build a tower, we should estimate the expenses and our ability to meet the payments. This is what Dietrich Bonhoeffer would call spelling out the cost of discipleship.

Individualism

A second aspect of American life that poses problems for the formation of religious identity is individualism. This is not to be confused with individuality, an unconditionally desirable trait which enables us to think for ourselves, resist pressures to conform, and take responsibility for our beliefs and commitments. Individualism, on the other hand, is a doctrine or attitude which assumes that only the individual, and not society, is what counts. Individual initiative, action, and interests should be independent of social control. According to this mentality, all values, rights, and duties originate only in individuals, and not in the social whole.

Taking this approach to religion is typically American; but, as Robert Bellah points out, it is at odds with the Jewish and Christian view of how we come to faith:

> The traditional pattern assumes a certain priority of the religious community over the individual. The community exists before the individual is born and will continue after his or her death. The relationship of the individual to God is ultimately personal, but is mediated by a whole pattern of community life. There is a givenness about the community and tradition. They are not normally a matter of individual choice.[4]

Most of the young people with whom we deal find it hard to open themselves to the notion of religious faith as a response to God's gratuitous revelation and a willingness to shape our beliefs and behavior in obedience to that revelation. Many of them find a kindred spirit in Sheila, a young woman who has named her religion after herself. She says: "I believe in God. I'm not a religious fanatic. I can't remember the last time I went to church. My faith has carried me a long way. It's Sheilaism. Just my own little voice."[5] Like her,

> [t]he students enrolled in our schools . . . nearly all believe in God. They avoid religious fanaticism like the plague. They hardly ever go to church. And their "faith" is little

more than listening to their own little voice, or rather to
the voices who tell them what they want to hear.[6]

They are not very different from most of their elders either.
William McCready, who has noted the reluctance of most Americans to heed moral imperatives, describes what he calls a major
change in the nation's religious character. For growing numbers
of people, he says, an individual search for meaning has become
the central religious experience.[7] And the impact on their moral
attitudes is profound. The influence of this kind of individualism
on religious practise and moral judgment is illustrated by these
two statements of eleventh graders:

> I don't think we need to go to church every Sunday as
> long as we have faith. . . . I believe in God and Jesus with
> all my heart but . . . I don't need the Church to tell me
> what I believe. Nor do I need the Church to enhance my
> faith. I am very independent and I don't think that I don't
> need God but I do believe that the Church is unnecessary
> or at least their rituals are. I think that my faith is more
> important to me because it comes from my heart; it is not
> dictated to me from a lectern every Sunday.

> I am a devout Christian who never misses Sunday Mass,
> [but] I believe that the Church is getting itself into some-
> place it doesn't belong when the priest uses the time for
> the homily to speak out on abortion. They are not politi-
> cians and have never had to worry about getting an abor-
> tion. They shouldn't be passing judgment on their neigh-
> bor. (I believe the Bible mentions that somewhere.)

Dealing with this individualistic strain in American youth
challenges the adult to be responsive and adaptive to this mentality and yet to be faithful to the Christian message. That is
more easily said than done. Fidelity requires a gentle insistence
on the legitimate demands of community, even while encouraging the thrust toward individuality that accompanies emotional
maturation. Fear of rejection can tempt us to soft-pedal unpopular truths, but we should try to be as kind and firm as Jesus was
in passing on hard sayings. The minister's duty is to try to be

heard and accepted, but, even more, to be honest. God does not oblige us to be successful, only to be faithful.

McCready estimates that about a third of the Roman Catholics in this country rarely or never go to church, yet they think of themselves as Catholics. The younger generation does not seem likely to reverse that trend. There is no easy solution to the problem of neglect of the Church's sacramental life, but pretending that the problem doesn't exist is no answer either. We must do our best to inculcate respect for tradition and to present faith as a response to a call, not a choice made in a vacuum.

Inadequate Images of God and Jesus

Religious attitudes and practices are intimately bound up with and influenced by subjective perceptions of God. For Christians the same can be said of the way Jesus is pictured and thought of. The influence is probably in both directions; images produce attitudes, that is, and attitudes modify images. By listening closely to the ways they describe God and Jesus, youth ministers can learn much about the faith of young people and about their religious needs and capacities.

Listen to what these four high-school girls say about God, both directly and by implication. The focus of their remarks is not God but two moral issues. The first two are explaining why they reject the Church's teaching against premarital sex, and the next two argue against the Church's condemnation of abortion:

God gave us life and told us he would not stand in the way, and would let us make our own decisions. Individuals should be the ones to dictate to themselves what their opinion on premarital sex is.

The Church can guide us, not tell us to say no, because the ultimate decision is ours alone.

I do believe in abortion. Everything goes back to the word "choice." As an individual you have the choice of how you want to do things in life. I think that God made everyone different, meaning everyone has a mind of their own to make decisions for themselves.

I see that God forgives you for your sins, so why is there such a big argument over abortion being wrong?

Obviously, much more than God-talk is going on here. The way these young people think about moral judgments and decision making is very revealing, and we shall return to that aspect a bit later. For now, though, consider what they say and imply about God. They are very clear—and quite correct—in thinking of God as one who brings us into existence, makes us all individuals, and scrupulously respects the freedom of will with which he endowed us. So far, so good. But then the implication is clear: This God not only makes us free but is also totally unconcerned about the way we use that freedom. Whatever we do is all right with God as long as we do it freely.

What we have here is a kind of moral deism, where God's only function is to set the world going and remain completely uninvolved The God of judgment has disappeared; what remains is a kind of cosmic Cheshire cat who, no matter what happens on earth, no matter what horrors we inflict upon one another, can only summon up a vapid, disembodied smile.

Where did this care-nothing God come from? Certainly not from Scripture, though some careless people still try to perpetuate the false dichotomy of an Old Testament God of judgment and a New Testament God of love. The only cure for this kind of myopia is to read the Bible itself, and not selected passages only. The Jewish Scriptures are replete with tender imagery of God as lover, most notably in Hosea, Ezekiel, and the Song of Songs. And in the New Testament Jesus repeatedly describes a God who is not only loving and forgiving but who also reminds us of the destructive consequences of sin. But, of course, those putting together the youth-group or class liturgy seldom choose passages such as these for their readings. Many young Catholics have probably never even heard or read them.

The current strange version of God may be the product of a new paganism, one that is intolerant of any restraint but loath to abandon the trappings and afterimages of the Judeo-Christian tradition. Remember McCready's observation, "Americans do not respond to moral imperatives." Surely this carefree creator is made to order for a culture whose dominant myth assures us that we should experience whatever we desire. One is reminded of H. Richard Niebuhr's devastating summary of a certain kind of relaxed Christianity: "A God without wrath brought people without sin into a kingdom without judgment through the ministrations of a Christ without a cross."[8]

Others see the origin of this doddering deity in certain trends of youth ministry in the past quarter of a century. In the warm afterglow of the Second Vatican Council, there was an overreaction against some preconciliar practices. The sterile legalism and minimalism, the neo-Puritanical preoccupation with sex, and the pervasiveness of a sometimes-irrational guilt provoked a rebellion of sorts against fear and guilt in any form. Religion teachers and retreat directors, determined not to subject their charges to the old, discredited guilt trips, exiled the God who was Creator, Lord, and Judge and enthroned in his place the Friend, Lover, and Companion. This was a God who, instead of frightening kids, would inspire them. Instead of reminding them of their failings, he would assure the young of their inherent goodness. God does not make junk.

Best of all, he would offer them unconditional love. Could he somehow provide more effectively what every adolescent needs, a positive self-image? But unconditional love on God's part, though a consoling reality, is easily misunderstood. Those who spoke of it to the young meant, quite rightly, that no matter what we do, God never stops loving us. But some heard instead that God loves us so much that he does not care what we do. A small mistake, with large consequences! And so we have the spectacle of Catholic adolescents arguing for premarital sex and abortion, and appealing to a God who has given them freedom with no strings attached.

How should the youth minister speak of God? The way Jesus does. As a loving, caring, forgiving parent who comforts us, his children. Also as a responsible parent who challenges us, has high hopes for us, is sometimes disappointed with us—a parent who must put limits on us for our own and our neighbors' (God's other children's) good. Good parents are not pushovers, and God is an infinitely good parent.

The images that young people have of Jesus are also vitally important. The most appealing one is that of Friend. At an age when friendship and acceptance are so important, the young find this a rich and authentic approach to intimacy with God's Son. But, as in the case of God, we must take care not to allow one aspect of a many-sided Person, no matter how attractive, to overshadow other qualities to the point of distortion. William O'Malley reminds us of this when he warns against making Jesus a kind of Warm Fuzzy, a doting sentimentalist whose only preoccupation is patting our little heads and assuring us that all is well even when it isn't. Real friends sometimes tell us things we don't like to hear, and Jesus is the best friend we'll ever have.

During the years when God and Jesus were having their images refurbished by well-meaning but myopic catechists and preachers, the late Gustave Weigel playfully remarked that hell seemed to be getting cooler every year. Whatever happened to hell anyway? Today, in many youth-ministry circles, it is treated the way we used to deal with dirty words: if we hear people mention it, we wash out their mouths with soap. And yet Monika Hellwig observes quite rightly that every page of the New Testament reminds us that everything is at stake in the way human beings use their freedom. The imagery and the details of hell are negotiable, of course; but not the note of urgency that comes through in Jesus' impassioned summons to renounce evil and embrace goodness.

It is this sense of urgency that often fails to come through in much of today's best-intentioned service of the young. The reasons are not hard to find. Sin and guilt and repentance are not very popular themes today. Talking about them in church or classroom or on retreat can earn low marks from young hearers who file all such topics under "fire and brimstone"—the ultimate put-down. But when we avoid such matters, salvation (from what?) becomes a game that no one can lose. And what could be more boring than that? Jesus was accused of many things in his time, but never of being boring. As I have pointed out elsewhere, the Jesus we meet in the Gospels

> is neither neutral nor nondirective. He doesn't tell his hearers that their main job is to find out what's important *for them*, or that their value judgements and choices are self-justifying so long as they feel good about them.

This Jesus is a well-kept secret. It's about time we blew his cover.

Notions of Morality

The fourth issue with which effective youth ministry must come to grips is the difficulty of communicating the moral dimension of the Gospel. There is a paradox here. Most young people are intensely curious about moral questions—the more controversial, the better. But several factors operative in the adult world as well as among the young can make it extremely difficult to carry on the most rudimentary dialogue. There is the unwillingness already alluded to, to respond to moral imperatives, an unwillingness so characteristic of this country. Moral relativism, long entrenched in secular academia, has its devotees among both the washed and the unwashed, for whom all moral strictures are arbitrary impositions. Telling others that, on the basis of moral grounds, they should or should not be doing something constitutes "imposing morality"—the biggest no-no of them all; for "right" and "wrong" exist only in the eye of the beholder.

Although teens and young adults often talk like moral relativists, appearances can be deceiving. They may well be reacting in an incoherent way to what they perceive as the high-handed, unfair, insensitive uses of authority by adults in power.

> "Who's to say" and "That's just your opinion" are clumsy ways of rejecting the idea that moral judgements derive their validity just from being said by authorities. "It's wrong to condemn others" is a reaction against the bullying tactics of judgmentalism, incautiously directed at

judgement in general. "If it's right for him, it's right" is a recognition of the plurality of the good (although misleadingly framed in terms of the right).[9]

Whether or not they are really relativists, however, they can be very hard to teach. And make no mistake about it: they very much need to learn. One does not have to be a prophet of gloom to see that our children are coming of age in an increasingly dangerous environment. Drugs, casual sex, pregnancy, abortion, and AIDS are only the most spectacular of the traps that await the unwary and inexperienced. "Youth at risk" has become a cliché. So the ability to make sound moral judgments and decisions holds a high priority, but it is becoming harder and harder to attain.

Recall the classroom conversation with which this chapter began. For as long as we can remember, creative teachers have resorted to some version of the moral dilemma in order to teach in an inductive way. The adult lays out the hypothetical case, indicates the options, and then asks, What should the person do? For years, the student would select one of the courses of action open to the subject, the teacher would ask why, and the group would go on its Socratic way to learn outcomes that were more or less enlightening. But over the course of the last few years, the conversation is likely to go more or less like the one described earlier:

TEACHER: . . . So those are the choices open to her. What should she do?

STUDENT: It's up to her.

TEACHER: Yes, I know it's up to her. So what should she do?

STUDENT: It's her choice.

TEACHER: *[Taking a deep breath to avoid losing his temper]*
Yes, we know it's her choice. But how should she choose? And on what grounds?

STUDENT: It's her choice.

What brought on this development? Among other factors, the abortion controversy has certainly contributed to it. Although there are arguments for abortion in certain circumstances and these deserve serious consideration, many pro-abortion adults short-circuited the national debate about the rights of the unborn by calling themselves "pro-choice." And so we and our children are being treated to something new under the sun, a dispute about a moral issue in which one side makes no arguments for the justice of its position, appealing instead simply to the right to choose. Thus we have on a national scale the same kind of frustrating non-conversation as the classroom dialogue described above. All pretense at rationality has been abandoned; the individual conscience has been pronounced infallible. In the face of an enormous and growing social evil, all that good citizens can do, we are told, is to leave one another alone. Is it any wonder that our children find it difficult to engage in meaningful moral discourse?

Despite these disheartening developments, however, there is much that youth ministers can do to help the young escape from the morass of confusion and self-deception. One of the most rewarding features of teaching adolescents is the opportunity to work with hearts that have not had time to harden and minds that are too young to be closed. Of course, they can be prickly and defensive too, and quite trying in many other ways. But for the patient, caring, and resourceful teacher or youth leader, there are great opportunities to win over hearts and minds. Grace builds on nature; and, while the young are limited in maturity and wisdom, they nearly always possess a bedrock openness and idealism waiting to be built upon.

The adult who wins the respect and confidence of the young and gains a hearing can contribute to moral development in ways too numerous to detail. But here are a few suggestions, which many of our readers will be able to expand upon from their own experience.

1. Expose the fallacy of the pro-choice argument. Point out that every choice is for something which can be helpful or destructive. When we catch muggers, drug dealers, and rapists, we impose our morality on them and put them in jail. We penalize them for exercising their freedom of choice by preying on their neighbors.

When confronted with arguments like these, of course, most kids don't just roll over.

STUDENT: That's different!

TEACHER: How? How are mugging and drug dealing and rape different?

STUDENT: They're illegal.

TEACHER: Good point! You're right. So what do you think? Is everything that is legal also right, and everything illegal thereby wrong?

The teacher and students can then explore together familiar examples from history. Did slavery become wrong only after the Emancipation Proclamation? Was denying women the vote wrong only after the passage of the Nineteenth Amendment? Helping black slaves escape via the underground railroad was illegal; so was hiding Anne Frank from the Nazis. Was it wrong? Interning Japanese-American citizens living near the Pacific coast in 1942 was legal; was it right? As of this writing, apartheid is the law of the land in South Africa; is it right?

Conversations like these can help youngsters who are thinking about such matters for the first time, who may never have heard of these events or were never encouraged to think about them in these ways. Even when, like those who would not listen to Stephen, they stop their ears and figuratively stone the teacher, the experience of such dialogue with its spur to critical thinking can be salutary in the long run.

2. Another way we can serve young people is to help them think out and imagine the consequences of their actions before they happen. Here are a boy and a girl thinking out loud about premarital sex:

> Most teenagers agree that haphazard premarital sex is wrong, but in cases where there is an intimate relationship, sex is a beautiful thing and can be engaged in, even though there may be consequences.

> I think that parents today have no concept of how truly close two young people can be. Parents just don't think that it's possible for a guy and a girl to be deeply committed to each other.

The inexperience and naivete of these otherwise-bright young people jump off the page and cry out for some reality therapy. They do not need to be preached to; rather, they need to explore with the help of a caring older person just what "consequences" and "commitment" and "responsibility" entail in real life. Someone must explain the basis of Christian sexual morality, not as an arsenal of arbitrary taboos, but as a respect for the demands of reality, for persons, and for new life. Someone has to answer the girl who wrote:

> I don't think it is up to the Church to put the label "wrong" on something as personal as sex. . . . The Church believes in suffering for one's God (because we love him so much)—and *how* they make young men and women suffer! The guilt they place on those who even *consider* premarital sex is enough to inhibit them for the rest of their lives! The Catholic Church is not to *impose* their views as they do, on anyone. God can be the only judge—and he forgives everyone—doesn't he? Or is the Church and its views a jumbled-up mess???

3. One inescapable conclusion from all this is that youngsters need help in learning how to form their consciences. Awareness of cultural and peer pressures, ideas of God, distinctions between temptation and sin, the limits of freedom, and the nature of responsibility are a big order for inexperienced young people growing up in a confused society, where amorality is normative and many consider uninhibited self-expression an absolute right.

4. More than clear thinking, however, is needed. As Craig Dykstra reminds us, moral agents are more than thinking persons; they are feeling, hoping, fearing persons.[10] There is an affective component in all moral decision making; the heart is engaged as well the head. In the case of young people, with their felt need for acceptance and belonging, peers play an important role in making value judgments. The negative influence of peer pressure is well recognized, but what is not always appreciated is the positive impact that peer pressure can have. Sometimes students will put in writing sentiments that challenge the prevailing pseudo-wisdom of their contemporaries. They often have a salutary effect on their young hearers simply because they are not perceived as speaking for the adult establishment. Here, for example, are some eleventh-graders speaking up for sexual responsibility:

BOY: Teenage love is an infatuation. Teenagers experience deep emotional, social, and psychological stress during these years. When viewed with hindsight, what is love to them one day can be the result of a massive hormone influx. Teenagers still have a long way to go before they are ready for real love.

GIRL: If two people love each other that much, why don't they get married? If they are too young, they are too young to handle such a big responsibility of the consequences after that. Also, when you make such a decision to make love to someone, you have to ask yourself these questions: Does he love me.? Is this a one-night stand? Is he forcing me? If two people love each other, they won't mind waiting until they are married. I know I will not engage in premarital sex. When I get married that is going to be one thing that I give my husband, something that no one else has and can take away.

BOY: I have lived with the pain. I have been through what everyone else brags about. It is not that good. In fact, it stinks. Don't get me wrong. I am not turned off by sex. I just feel that there is a time for everything, and it is up to the individual to control his desires. Young people don't realize that sex can make their lives permanently changed.

GIRL: *[Commenting on this last statement]*

Experience is the best teacher. This guy sounds like he knows what he is talking about. Many other teenagers should follow his advice.

Exercises like these are helpful to adolescents because they show how divided they and their peers are on these matters. This may seem like a small accomplishment, but it is important. Otherwise, they might assume that it's an "us against them" situation, where adults defend traditional values and young people are all naysayers. Exposing the divisions among the young helps them to see that, in order to take a stand, they must do more than choose up sides in a phony intergenerational war.

And it is worth the effort. Sometimes persistence pays off, as in the case of the boy who wrote this at the end of the year:

When we began the sexuality part of this course, I thought it would be a grand waste of time. For what could there be that I, a teenager, did not know about? My mind seemed to be a closed door, shut tight by the security that all teens seem to possess. Over this past weekend, I have looked over some of my homeworks, which often had comments [by the teacher] which I did not want to accept. Most of these things I just laughed at and put in my folder. But after reading them all together I felt strange. I felt as if I was the one who almost wasted his time by keeping my mind closed. I was scared. Scared to be a teenager in an age of AIDS, VD, and abortion, in a society which often does not provide support or help to those who most need it. Most teens have kept their minds closed to the ideas and precautions of adults who, whether we like it or not, know more about life than we do.

My only problem bigger than my closed mind during this course was my closed heart. My view on abortion was that it didn't matter. Let women and girls do what they want as long as I don't have to feel any pain, any remorse, or any regret. I had a Superman-like aura around me. I didn't think about what I was saying when I said that things were not going to affect me. Maybe it takes the fear of being a teen in today's society to open up minds and, more importantly, hearts.

One of my problems has been that I was afraid of what seems to be a majority around me. Most of my friends engage in sex and I'm afraid to seem out of line or conservative. But over this weekend I have come to a strong conviction within myself. . . . I feel better about myself and about others. I feel that I can help to change things and that I can make a difference (however small) in our world. I look forward to the chance of helping a friend to decide not to have sex or not to have an abortion. These are terrible problems but my weaknesses have been replaced with strengths. My mind, body, and heart are one and ready to face society and hopefully make a change.

Notions of Religion

The last issue to be considered in our survey of the problems and possibilities of youth ministry is the nature of young people's religious aspirations and strivings. When we take an explicitly religious approach to young people, how do they perceive us? What are their expectations and felt needs? How do these compare with our own self-understanding and priorities?

As usual, there is good news and bad news. The good news is that the vast majority of the young people we meet in our various ministries are basically religious, at least in the sense of being open to a religious message. This should not surprise us, since the American people are surely more religious than the popular organs of mass entertainment would have us believe. As we heard from the deprogrammer cited earlier (pp. 11-12) young people are looking for idealism, community, and a sense of belonging. As one would expect, however, this religious receptivity is accompanied by a good deal of ambivalence. A high school junior, asked why the number of Catholic priests is declining, wrote:

> When boys grow up, they see that the people who are enjoying (or seem to enjoy) life are the well-off people. The work they do to go to a good college, they don't want to waste on a life of little means as a priest. They want to be worth something. People are too greedy and possessive.

It is not clear where this student stands. What does he mean by "being worth something"? He seems to suspect that materialism may be bankrupt, but doesn't know what to put in its place. He senses that something has gone wrong, but sees no other way to go.

Of course, there is bad news, too. Like their elders, many young Americans are inclined to reduce the religious quest to the search for a congenial cult, a comfortable code, and a compatible community. The temptation to invent their own brand of Sheilaism, the do-it-yourself religion of the young woman quoted earlier (p. 136) will always be there as long as religious individualism and consumerism are around. Teenagers especially, with their need to be accepted and to blend in, are liable to find prophetic religion frightening. It appears that many of those who minister to them have decided not to frighten them. Hence the God who wants whatever they want, and Jesus the pal who makes no demands. But there is a side of youth that welcomes risk and challenge too, and this should not be ignored.

Adolescents are different from adults in so many ways that it is not surprising that their ways of "doing" religion should be different too. Some of the differences are insignificant, due simply to passing phases in their growing up, and involve only superficial matters of style. For example, several years ago it had to be explained to skeptical adults that, when teens sat on the floor at Mass, it was their way of expressing, not casualness, but reverence. Time takes care of such minor misunderstandings, but a few merit closer attention, if only to help the generations communicate better. Among these are their attitudes toward obligation, spontaneity, routine, and celebration.

Among large numbers of the young, the idea of performing some religious activity out of a sense of obligation meets with an intensely negative response. Something in the adolescent psyche, which this writer does not pretend to understand completely, judges very harshly anyone who would participate in the liturgy out of a sense of duty. This strikes them as inauthentic and phony. As one boy wrote,

> Why aren't Masses optional anyway? We've discussed why man sins and we decided that, without the freedom to sin, being good means nothing. If Mass is mandatory, then it defeats its own purpose. Most people will go because they have to, and they come out feeling the same way without ever gaining knowledge or ever enhancing their faith.

Some may ascribe this phenomenon simply to the well-known resistance of adolescents to rules. But this does not explain why earlier generations of teenagers accepted the Sunday obligation in theory if not in practice. Whatever the explanation may be, the youth minister is well advised to tread carefully in this area. For reasons that may be more cultural than psychological, today's young people equate integrity with spontaneity. This goes beyond the obligation to celebrate the Eucharist. The idea of setting aside certain times of the day for prayer is also considered inauthentic. If you pray or worship for any other reason than that you *feel* like doing it right here and now, you are just going through the motions, and your prayer is worthless. Is such thinking shallow and immature? Of course it is. But that's what you have to contend with if you throw in your religious lot with the young.

Their attitudes toward prayer and worship have one more twist which creates a good deal of anxiety among adults who try to share faith with them. This is the problem, already alluded to from several different angles, of young people's neglect of the sacraments, especially the Eucharist. This argument has been going on for so long now that both sides are growing weary of it and are making overtures toward what looks more and more like an uneasy truce. "They made a desert and called it peace." But before giving up, it may be worth considering some elements that have received insufficient attention.

Everyone has heard over and over again why kids (and some adults) don't go to Mass. "It was boring." "I didn't get anything out of it." First of all, what do they want to get out of it? An immediate, palpable, emotional return on their investment of time and attention. When liturgy goes well and every person and thing comes together, we have a conscious feeling of self-improvement, a sense that our active faith has been enhanced. Everyone, not just teenagers and young adults, wants this to happen in church. It ought to happen more often, and we should all work a little harder to make it happen. No quarrel here. What is troubling is the corollary: If these things *don't* happen, then *nothing* happens. The whole exercise is worthless. "I got *nothing* out of it."

These are hard sayings for those of us who grew up believing that, even when prayer and worship, including the Eucharist, were less than inspiring, Christ was truly present, God's grace was operative, and the reception of Holy Communion was of immense value. This is not to be misinterpreted as a hankering after the return of *ex opere operato* rationalizations of humdrum or sloppy liturgy. I am simply pointing out that religion teachers have their work cut out for them when they try to inculcate an appreciation of and a reverence for the sacraments of the Church. Religious illiteracy takes many forms; one of them is an impoverished understanding of the sacraments.

Where did this almost intractable mentality come from? According to James Heft, the new religious receptivity of adolescents suffers from an absorption in the self. They demand that all spirituality must be rooted in human experience and must somehow be related to self-development. These demands are not unreasonable, but they do run the risk of getting lost in self-absorption and of being separated from religion's communal dimension, from metaphysical considerations, and from history. He cites the theory, developed by Philip Rieff in *The Triumph of the Therapeutic*,[11] of long-range characterological changes in the

West. According to Rieff, the old ideals were the political person, the religious person, and the economic person. What has been emerging for the last few decades is a new ideal, the psychological person, who rejects all forms of commitment except the pursuit of one's own well-being. For this type the highest good is entertainment, and the greatest evil is boredom.

How do I respond to such a mentality? I try to help my students see beyond short-term goals as they evaluate their sacramental encounters by reflecting with them on their experiences of learning in school. Do they feel smarter at 3 P.M. than they did at 9 A.M.? Wiser on Friday than on the previous Monday? No, they answer. Are most of their classes humdrum and forgettable? Yes, is their reply. And yet, isn't it strange that between September and May, if they hang in there and make an effort, something wonderful takes place. They learn. They grow. Talents develop. Skills are honed. Slowly, imperceptibly, but no less dramatically, maturity happens. That is the way God works too. We must not look for immediate, perceptible results from our sacramental meetings with Christ. That is like checking a plant every day to see if it has grown. Relationships need time to develop and deepen, and they are nourished by fidelity and perseverance; my relationship with Christ is no different.

Self-development, of course, is not the only norm by which to judge our sacramental life. But it is, not surprisingly, the one that seems to mean most to adolescents. And we can appeal to this dimension without distorting the reality.

Conclusion

When those of us who minister to the young encounter the mentalities and attitudes described in these pages, we have to make pastoral decisions based not only on responsiveness to youth's felt needs and expectations but also on fidelity to the message of Christ. The same challenge faces those of us who do not work with youth but who encounter adult versions of these same problems. What is negotiable and what is nonnegotiable?

When does fidelity become rigidity, and when does accommodation become betrayal?

Tevye, the protagonist in the popular musical *Fiddler on the Roof*, tries to adapt to a changing world when modernity makes its way into his remote Russian village. Love of his growing daughters moves him, a pious orthodox Jew, to make one concession after another to the new worldview which they and their young suitors represent. In each instance we hear the refrain, "On the one hand (I shouldn't) . . . but on the other hand (I'll give in this time)." At length, when one daughter violates the great taboo and asks permission to marry a Gentile, her father proclaims, "There is no other hand!" But it is too late. Tevye's beliefs have died the death of a thousand qualifications. As the story ends the family goes into exile to escape a pogrom. But their final status as wanderers in a strange land only mirrors the spiritual breakup of their world that had begun years before.

If we ourselves are disciples and not just religious consumers, we will have to come to terms with the fact that we are out of step with much of what goes on in American life. The youngsters who just want to "eat good, look good, and smell good" are not against religion as long as it doesn't challenge their values or interfere with their plans. But if we are going to teach as Jesus did, then part of the Gospel we announce must be a call to conversion. Never, perhaps, were both young and old less inclined to heed such a call; never was it needed more.

If all we want is to be liked by all our kids, we will have to stay away from the hard sayings. Many of our young people do not want to be told that consumerism is a shallow way of life, that religion is a community affair, that the Eucharist is a nonnegotiable element of Christian life, that you can't write off the Church and call yourself a Catholic, that God not only loves them but also makes demands, that Jesus is more than a pal, that some of their moral choices might be wrong, that premarital sex is not a right, that social justice is not optional, that religion is not a consumer item, that we are called to measure up to what God wants, not the other way around. It's much safer to keep it general, to tell them that they're beautiful, that God loves them just the way they are, and to leave them with the impression that whatever they do is all right with God just as long as they want to do it. The hard sayings will lose us followers, just as they cost Jesus many of his disciples.

Such skills are much needed today. Many of our fellow Americans young and old have been sold a way of life that is in many respects shallow, exploitative, and ultimately unsatisfying. Remember, it took a child to notice and say out loud that the emperor had no clothes on. The children who have spoken to us in these pages are trying to get our attention, and, as Mrs. Loman said in *Death of a Salesman,* attention must be paid.

Topics for Discussion

1. Compare the religious consumerism of the young with that of adults.

2. Are teenagers more vulnerable than adults to the influence of consumerism?

3. How do you explain to someone, young or old, that morality is more than a point of view?

4. Is it possible for religious education to blunt the impact of the dominant culture?

Notes

1. Deidre Carmody, "To Freshmen, A Big Goal Is Wealth," *New York Times,* 14 Jan. 1988.

2. "Still Killing Us Softly," Cambridge Documentary Files.

3. Cited in film guide, "The Thirty Second Dream," Mass Media Ministries.

4. Robert Bellah et al., *Habits of the Heart* (New York: Harper & Row, 1985), 227.

5. Ibid., 221.

6. James J. DiGiacomo, *Teaching Religion in a Catholic Secondary School* (Washington, D.C.: National Catholic Educational Association, 1989), 1.

7. Kenneth A. Briggs, "Religious Feeling Seen Strong in U.S.," *New York Times,* 9 Dec. 1984.

8. H. Richard Niebuhr, *The Kingdom of God in America,* Harper Torchbook (New York: Harper & Row, 1959), 193. I have changed Niebuhr's "man" to "people."

9. Robert Fullinwider, "The Menace of Moral Relativism," reprint (Center for Philosophy and Public Policy, 1987).

10. Craig Dykstra, *Vision and Character* (New York: Paulist Press, 1981), 7-11.

11. New York: Harper & Row, 1966.

Afterword

THE HISTORY OF RELIGIOUS EDUCATION IN THE LAST 25 YEARS AND the present situation offer us a scene of heartening achievements, nagging disappointments, and unfinished business. The religious formation of the young has made great strides. Professionalism among religious educators and other youth ministers is much advanced. Publishers in the religious education field are turning out materials quite superior to those of a generation ago. Young people themselves are far more receptive to religion and religious experience. The strident alienation of the late 60s and the early 70s is now a distant memory. There is a flourishing retreat movement that features many different approaches to youth's religious needs and capacities. Many schools have upgraded their religion programs and made them more academically respectable.

There have also been some disappointments. Michael Warren's challenge of a decade ago, to integrate religious education with other elements of youth ministry, has yet to be met. There is a lack of congruence between the religious knowledge of young people and their religious experience and practise, between what is learned in the classroom and what happens in the retreat house. In away-from-school retreats, students experience affirmation and encouragement. They are helped to open up to one another, to experience acceptance and trust and friendship. They pray and worship together in ways that often inspire them and send them back to their homes with revived enthusiasm, a feeling of having been spiritually renewed. But we are left with some questions. Do these retreat experiences help them to overcome exaggerated religious individualism, to pray regularly, to participate in the sacramental life of the church? Do they meet the Jesus and the God of Christian tradition? Are they helped to come to terms with the larger Christian community? Is there any vital link forged between religious knowledge and day-to-day practise?

There are many reasons why it is difficult to integrate religious literacy and sentiment. Many of the most accurate and faithful presentations of the Christian message fail to confront and deal effectively with certain elements in the modern mentality that militate against comprehension and internalization. Among the most intractable of these are individualism, moral relativism, and consumerism. Young people who are profoundly affected by these patterns of thought and aspiration tend to filter out those aspects of the Gospel which clash with the presuppositions of the dominant culture. And for those who wish to get a hearing with the young, the temptation is strong to omit altogether these less appealing dimensions of the Gospel.

Anyone who has not only been talking to teenagers for the last 25 years but also carefully listening to them will recognize the following Creed which is hereby published for the first time. It is the operative belief system of innumerable young people, including many who have had the benefit of religious education in Catholic institutions. I call it:

"Brand X" Religion

I believe in God.

I believe in Jesus.

Everyone is allowed to follow whatever religion he/she chooses. No one can say one religion is better than any other. The way to pick a religion is to find one that agrees with your way of thinking.

We have a choice of praying to God by ourselves or with other people. If worshipping God with other people is boring or if we don't get anything out of it, then we don't have to do it. Ultimately, it doesn't matter what you believe as long as you are good.

In order to be good, just follow your conscience and do what you think is right. No one can tell anyone else what is right or wrong, since it all depends on how you look at it.

This individualistic, relativistic religion bears little resemblance to the Gospel, but retains just enough of the after-images and trappings of Christianity to pass as an up-to-date version of the real thing. It appeals to those who are frightened by the cost of discipleship and would like to settle for some kind of religious consumerism. There have always been well-meaning but superficial people who treat religion not as a summons to transcendence but as a product to be consumed or not, depending on the buyer's felt needs.

Not all young people subscribe to this formless brand of religious consumerism. Most of them are still open to idealism and challenge. But they need help to sort out the wheat from the chaff. They need to hear the whole Gospel, not just the popular, comforting passages that leave complacency undisturbed. The differences between Christianity and the various forms of "Brand X" religion have to be spelled out. The dominant culture must be analyzed and critiqued, and its unspoken premises brought to consciousness.

Religious educators and catechists are faced with a task much like the one that confronted their counterparts in ancient Rome. They had to tell their catechumens that they were faced with a clear choice: either live like the other Romans, or subscribe to a whole new way of life. It is becoming increasingly clear that Christianity today is countercultural. Although there are many fine and wonderful things in the American way of life, there are also patterns of judgment and conduct and underlying values that are simply irreconcilable with the following of Christ. If we don't present our religion, more and more explicitly, as a competing formula for happiness and fulfillment, we will see repeated an incident that happened recently to a Catholic high school religion teacher. One of his twelfth graders who had taken a course in world religions announced that he liked Catholicism best, because "you don't have to *do* anything."

We do not have to deny any of the good things that have been happening in youth ministry in the last 25 years, to acknowledge that much remains to be done. Here is a checklist of things that religious educators need to tell the young for at least the next 25 years:

1. Consumerism is a shallow and ultimately unsatisfying way of life.

2. Religion is a community affair. We cannot do it alone.

3. The Eucharist is essential to the Christian life.

4. We cannot dismiss the Church and call ourselves Catholic.

5. God not only loves us but also makes demands.

6. Jesus is more than a pal.

7. Some of our moral choices may be wrong.

8. Premarital sex is not a right.

9. Working for social justice is not optional.

10. We must measure up to what God wants, not the other way around.

To many youngsters, these are hard sayings. If we spell out these costs of discipleship, we will turn some of them off. They do not want to be told that in order to be Catholic you have to *do* something. But the alternative is hardly acceptable to those who claim to teach as Jesus did. He got off a few hard sayings in his own time, and they cost him followers. We disciples are not above the master. Of course, we should not be harsh or needlessly confrontational. Jesus warned us not to break the bruised reed or quench the smoking flax. For some time now, the kids have not been used to hearing this sort of thing. But sooner or later we have to get on with the unfinished business of inviting them, bravely and honestly, to join us in the following of Christ.

Acknowledgments

The chapters of this book were originally published, in whole or in part, as follows:

"Why Johnny Can't Pray," *America*, Dec. 10, 1977.

"Follow Your Conscience," *The Living Light*, March, 1979.

"Moral Education of Youth: Task and Accomplishment," *New Catholic World*, July, 1978.

"Evangelizing the Young," *America*, Oct. 13, 1979.

"Will My Child Keep the Faith?," *Catholic Update*, August, 1980.

"The Catholic Educator as Minister," *Ministries*, September, 1980.

"Teaching the Next New Breed," *America*, June 27, 1981.

"Can Adolescents Express Faith in Worship?," *Modern Liturgy*, September, 1981.

"The Religious Needs of Teens," *Marriage and Family Living*, October, 1981.

"Telling the Jesus Story," *Today's Catholic Teacher*, November-December, 1981.

"The New Illiteracy," *Church*, Fall, 1986.

"All You Need Is Love," *America*, February 14, 1987.

"Schools and Moral Development," *Caring for America's Children*, Academy of Political Science, 1989.

"Ministering to the Young," *Studies in the Spirituality of Jesuits*, March, 1991.

"Catechesis and Youth: Where's the Beef?" *Living the Vision*, Silver Burdett Ginn, 1992.